LISTEN,

FEEL,

RESPOND

LISTEN, FEEL, RESPOND

A workbook and guide to acting on camera

Paul Neal Rohrer

iUniverse, Inc.
New York Lincoln Shanghai

LISTEN, FEEL, RESPOND
A workbook and guide to acting on camera

iUniverse books may be ordered through booksellers or by contacting:

iUniverse
2021 Pine Lake Road, Suite 100
Lincoln, NE 68512
www.iuniverse.com
1-800-Authors (1-800-288-4677)

ISBN-13: 978-0-595-35170-1 (pbk)
ISBN-13: 978-0-595-79869-8 (ebk)
ISBN-10: 0-595-35170-0 (pbk)
ISBN-10: 0-595-79869-1 (ebk)

Printed in the United States of America

Contents

Whether this book represents your first step or one of many, it is my hope and intention that you will be inspired to *listen* more deeply and more effectively and that what you hear are messages of success and fulfillment.

SPECIAL THANKS

When my good friend and business partner, Peter DeAnello suggested that I write a book about my coaching style and philosophy, I thought, "What a joke!" My entire life has been spent acting and coaching actors. I believe that writing is a skill best left to professionals; however, I am grateful for those who have urged me to write this book of instruction and for all of you who will forgive my literary shortcomings.

It is Peter's style to coach by example, so he first published the book entitled *Monologue from Mystery to Mastery*. It is a book every actor and every acting coach should own. It is by Peter's example, guidance and encouragement that I am able to share these ideas beyond the walls of my classroom and into the pages of this book.

Two students in particular deserve special thanks. Alan Shackelford and Nancy Fromhart agreed to meet me at the Copper Pot, a restaurant in a strip mall located in south Denver that serves Indian food, buffet style. The lunch rush (if there is one) had passed so we had the whole place to ourselves. The food was less than wonderful, but the support and direction that Alan and Nancy offered that day was enough to break the spell of inactivity and the first of these pages was begun.

Diane Thiemann and Sarah Sweet proved invaluable by working exercises as they were written and returned the worksheets with comments of support, encouragement, correction and praise.

Paul Blomquist is a good friend and dedicated student that helped in countless ways. Be on the lookout for anything he may put his name on in the future.

A special thank you goes to my beloved sister Naomi Rohrer for editing this book.

There are numerous others who accepted the challenge to read and support early drafts, and to all of you I am grateful.

To my bride of twenty-two years, I am especially grateful for the love, respect and encouragement that you have always given. The two remarkable children that we brought into this world continue to inspire and reward.

To the hundreds of students I have worked with over the years, you are the greatest inspiration and reason for this book. I look forward to the day when those of you who have stuck with it, will step up to that moment of success and embrace it deeply, fully and humbly.

FOREWORD

PAUL NEAL ROHRER is a thirty(plus)-year veteran of film, television and stage. Recipient of the honorable CLIO and EMMY award numerous times, he has been hired to perform for the Academy Award-Winning Producer Carol Pasternak, with Dewey-Obenchain Films, on various occasions.

Mr. Rohrer has studied with some of the most recognized and successful leaders of the film and television industry: Tony Barr, Lynn Stalmaster, Marvin Paige, Mike Fenton and Dabney Coleman to name a few. Mr. Bob Giraldi, (*Dinner Rush*) cast Paul Rohrer as Mr. Erikson, (a turn-of-the-century salesman of electricity) for McCann-Erikson's Pacific Gas & Electric commercial in 1982. This was the beginning of Mr. Rohrer's continued success in the commercial, film and video marketplace.

A professional on stage and for the camera since 1978, Mr. Rohrer is internationally recognized for his public speaking, acting and directorial skills for both public and private enterprises. Fortune 500 Companies, such as IBM, Sunoco Oil, Hewlett-Packard and Caterpillar are among the hundreds of industrial, commercial and feature-length film work to Mr. Rohrer's credit.

Students attend his weekly workshops in a studio setting where they learn all aspects of working as professionals on camera, as well as off. Mr. Rohrer is able to draw on his many years of experience and materials, in addition to the many industry-related professionals who also share their expertise as guests of the Rohrering Success Workshops.

Thank you for picking up yet another book on ACTING. I hope that you will continue to pick up book after book after book. No one person in any one field has all of the answers or all of the ways in which to create your greatness. William Shakespeare wrote, "…be not afraid of greatness: some are born great, some achieve greatness, and some have greatness thrust upon 'em." The power of that message suggests there is hope for success for everyone.

The ideas, methods and instruction on how to act for the camera are as numerous as the stars in the sky, or at least on the Hollywood walk of fame. That is why it is important for you to discover a process that works for you.

This book is designed to walk you through a system of thought, process and action, which at first may seem foreign, complicated and/or time-consuming.

The good news is you are already well equipped to master the ideas presented if you are an actor who seeks inspiration and challenge.

There are many other valuable and challenging books on how to act that examine and detail the classic methods, styles and techniques of The Method, Improvisation, Meisner, Stanislovski and so forth. Each of those styles has proven its value with the great students and masters of the technique. You may remember Stella Adler and Uta Hagen, who used the classic styles of training but were also able to discover, develop and train others with what they had discovered and developed as their own style.

It is my intent that this book will inspire, aid and prepare actors who are looking for more answers; not necessarily as a *better* way, but perhaps in a way that you have not yet explored. A way that will continue to inspire you, challenge you to ask more questions and endeavor to seek more answers.

Between these two cover pages I address three specific areas:

Part One of three is an introduction, in which I share some of my personal inspirations and reasons for getting started in this sometimes crazy and always challenging business of acting.

If you are reading this book, you have a dream. Like many people, you probably feel a need for some help in realizing your dream. You may be hesitant to take a step, paralyzed by the daunting road ahead. As in any other profession, the larger picture can be overwhelming. Yet by taking the first step, you are likely to take the next.

Whether this book represents your first step or one of many, it is my hope and intention that you will be inspired to *listen* more deeply and more effectively and that what you hear are messages of encouragement, appreciation, success and fulfillment.

Part Two is an introduction to my own coaching style that I refer to as:

Listen, Feel, Respond.

In the *Listen, Feel, Respond* work, I prefer not to suggest that it is a method or technique. It is more accurately referred to as a *style* (as in acting style or life style), since especially good acting is created through an exceptionally different lifestyle.

In part two, you will see a number of exercises that I developed and use in my workshops to strengthen the focus of *Listen, Feel, Respond*. Peruse and review these exercises as many times as you wish until they are familiar.

By developing the skills of *Listen, Feel, Respond*, you will greatly improve your public speaking, acting and personal life skills.

Part Three contains a number of tools you will need in order to be taken seriously in this business. The detailed information in this section about resumes, invaluable tips on headshots, a guide to finding agents, and even suggestions regarding mobile phones will give you an edge as an actor in today's marketplace.

One final section to this book is the glossary of terms. Just as with any specialized profession, there is a language that defines tools and actions with their own (seemingly) alien words and definitions. If, while reading through this book, you come upon a word or description that defies your current knowledge of the English language and its contents, perhaps the glossary will come in handy. I hope you will have some fun reading through the glossary and will be better informed by it.

Part One

CHAPTER ONE

THE ACT OF BECOMING IS DOING

My father is not only a jack of many trades; he has also mastered most of those trades he has practiced.

While developing a mastery of some of his trades, he had a shop larger than his living area. In his shops he had lathes, table saws, workbenches, folding tables, storage bins, shelves, rows of hand powered tools, electric powered tools, scissors powerful enough to cut your finger off (no, he hasn't yet), rolls of upholstery fabric, layers of stuffing, piles of wood, stacks of piping and much more.

Most of what we had in our home was crafted or repaired by my father. We had a base rocker that he made from scratch, custom designed for our mother who comfortably rocked all three of her children in that chair. Our sofa was perfectly reupholstered, several times, by Dad. Our homes were the neighborhood eyesore when he purchased them at *bargain basement* rates because they were in such a state of disrepair. Several months following, Dad would have the flooring, walls, wiring, cabinetry and fixtures torn out and replaced with solid, pre-owned materials that seemed better than new. The property value soared and the neighbors were happier than ever.

After working an eight-hour shift, the family would gather around a simple table, and Dad would bless whatever food was provided. Then back to work he would go, downstairs to his shop until it was time for bed. Six days a week, every week, this was his routine. I never heard him complain and we never went hungry or without our most basic needs. My father is loved, respected and honored by his entire family.

So why do I share that story of my father in a book about *acting*: a subject about which my father knows virtually nothing? Because I want you to see that success in any aspect of life, be it acting or providing for your family, is built upon a foundation formed of the same principles:

1. Be willing to do the work.

2. Use the best and most appropriate tools.

3. If there is something you don't know how to do, or you can't afford to pay somebody else to do it, *or you don't want anyone else to do it,* get busy and learn to do it yourself.

In 1985 when I first set foot in a workshop designed to train actors for the camera, I had seven years of professional stage experience and more than a dozen additional years of amateur experience and development under my belt. Boy was I was full of spit and vinegar!

Like so many who have come up in the theatre, I had overcome so many fears of giving live presentations in front of large groups. I had developed my memory skills by delivering the classics, as well as contemporary pieces. This experience took me far beyond the proscenium and into the audience with participatory children's theatre and numerous presentations in public schools, Theatre in the Park, performances in greenhouses, churches, and huge auditoriums.

I wore masks, body stockings, paint, rubber and liquid latex. I learned Japanese phonetically to be a camel-dragging warrior. I wore chicken feathers and stuffing to cluck and squawk at the top of my lungs, and raced up and down a 500-seat auditorium chasing a kangaroo while dressed as a dingo dog.

None of this could have prepared me for the tremendous demands the film and television industry would put upon me.

Most of us were introduced to acting in a public school program. Even though the hearts of our public educators may have been in the right place, they were limited in what they could teach us. By doing what they suggested, I was able to learn the basics of theatre history and performance, but very little that would help me to earn a living acting.

After looking around at what else was available, I auditioned for the Goodman School of Drama, in the days before it was owned by DePaul University.

Auditioning at this level, as a young man, was a feeling that is hard to describe. It was far and away above anything else I had ever experienced. From that point forward, I knew I would have to seek training only from the best informed and most adept at their craft.

> I believe that it is very important to be enrolled in a training program that puts you in personal contact with people who are practicing what they are teaching.

Did you ever have teachers who spent their time handing out assignments and delivering lectures from their desk or podium as though every word and every lesson was a chore? It was obvious they would prefer to be in their office at their desk, or anywhere other than in front of you and your peers. Every hour seemed like a lifetime as their recitations oozed out like molasses from a wide mouth jar. The thick, dark and sticky facts, formulas and information would be on the test at the end of the week. It seemed there was no other reason to pay attention to such drivel than to regurgitate it for the test.

Now, take a deep breath and recall the teachers or professors who stepped away from their desk or podium and spoke from their heart. They enjoyed sharing their passion for the subject. The lesson was more of a story or a list of interesting subjects as they were made to relate to you and your personal understandings. Taking time to seek out each student, they would speak to that student, looking her in the eyes, they would smile, knowing that she was listening to and understanding what they had to say.

CHAPTER TWO

The three intangible assets that will attract those who can elevate your abilities and opportunities to the highest levels of achievement are:

Passion, Charisma and Uniquity.

(Yes, *uniquity*...it is my unique way of saying uniqueness.)

Take a close look at each of these three elements, **Passion. Charisma. Uniquity.** They are what I believe to be the most important assets for an actor to have and to develop. They are more important than any talent or ability. These three key elements allow any producer or director to *see* whatever talent that actor may have.

PASSION *noun*: A **powerful emotion**, such as love, joy, hatred, or anger. *(The American Heritage® Dictionary of the English Language, Fourth Edition, © 2000, Houghton Mifflin Company.)* **Emotion** is a mental state related to mood, sometimes even identified with it. Emotions are generally considered to be more transient than moods.

CHARISMA *noun*: a personal attractiveness that enables you to influence others. *(WordNet ® 2.0, © 2003 Princeton University)* The word **Charisma** (from the Greek word *charis*, or gift) is often used to describe an ability to **charm or influence** people.

UNIQUITY *noun*: the quality of being **one of a kind**. *(Paul Rohrer, 2003, First Edition)* There is no one else like you; you have something to offer that is truly original and invaluable.

If you are able to charm or influence a casting director with a *one of a kind* delivery, revealing honest and powerful emotion, you will indeed have their undivided attention in whatever you have prepared.

Few people choose acting as a profession based solely on the financial rewards it might offer. Most actors are already passionate about their choice of professions and are relatively charismatic individuals. The most difficult element to develop in most cases is *to trust* and *believe in* your own **uniquity**.

> Understand that there never was, is not now, and never will be, anyone exactly like you. You are indeed unique to the entire world; Past, Present and Future. Cherish and nurture your uniquity!

As you search for answers about what it is that makes you unique, you will become amazingly **observant**.

WHAT DO YOU SEE?

Being observant requires the ability to dismiss, or at least *rearrange*, judgment. **When you dismiss judgment, you are able to *see* what otherwise is *invisible*.**

One of the most effective ways to develop your *uniquity* is to let go of or dismiss expectations and judgments in exchange for what YOU *feel* or understand. Your feelings and reactions are uniquely yours. Allow yourself the opportunity to own those feelings and emotions.

For example, when you exit the highway and are confronted with the person holding a ragged cardboard sign, what judgments do you make?

If you have been homeless and in need, would your judgment be different than if you have never personally come in contact with such a person? Now, consider letting go of what you think you know (or don't know) about such a person. Simply observe. In the time it takes before the light turns green, you will make discoveries and see things that before you took this *risk*, were unseen or invisible.

Let's compare what you observed before your eyes met, versus what you observed after your eyes met.

Did you see anything besides what was written on the cardboard? What other signs was this person holding? Could you see, or were your judgments blinding you? Was the person sad? Angry? Joyful? Grateful? Resolute? Did you see the emotion in his eyes? What details do you remember about his clothing? Was anybody else with him? What personal items did he have?

If you caught his eye or he yours, what happened then? Without question I know you were made to feel something. You felt it quickly, deeply and it changed your behavior immediately. Maybe you looked away, or smiled. You did something because you were made to feel something. Your reaction was swift and definite.

Now, imagine *you* are the person holding the sign, and a casting director is exiting the highway, about to look your way. Are you ready to meet her eyes?

The decisions of a casting director are made in much the same way. If someone has spoken well of you and your abilities before that casting director has ever been introduced to you, how do you think you will be judged? Would you be judged differently without that introduction? What if, six months earlier, you had made several memorable mistakes on her set, which had put them behind schedule?

There is no question that if everyone at every level of this industry were able to hire based solely on what occurs at the audition and *only* at the audition, there would be a huge difference in who and what we would see on the screen. However, that is neither feasible nor realistic.

It is industry standard to make comparisons and references to whom or what has already been successful, in order to draw attention and interest to a specific person or project.

It is the purpose and goal of each person and project to be unique enough to make drawing those comparisons difficult.

Therefore, it is up to every actor/artist to be as well-prepared as possible before putting oneself in a position to be judged and remembered. The best way to do that is to get perspective, information and training from qualified and successful sources.

On the other hand, any comparisons that are made must be successful ones.

Let's take for example, a writer who is pitching his latest project to an executive. When asked what his project is about, he explains, "My story is *Howard the Duck* meets *Zardoz*."

How interested do you think that executive will be in picking up that story?

I give Mr. Lucas the golden handshake on the majority of his work, but his *Howard the Duck* picture is one that falls far short of his obvious abilities. In addition, I am not sure Mr. Connery would ever wish to be remembered for *Zardoz*. Why would an executive invest in a project whose aim is to be like a box office fizzle?

In contrast, how would that executive perceive the value of a project presented to him as, say, "*Godfather* meets *Pulp Fiction*?" Their phenomenal success at the box office lends piazzaz to the possibilities and potential of your own project in comparison.

Consider the producer who asks the agent to be honest about her latest talent acquisition and the agent responds, "Bobby is like Telly Savalas with hair."

With respect to Mr. Savalas, who was magnificent as *Kojak*, being compared to an actor who had a limited repertoire is deadly. Now consider the actor who is able to take advantage of his unique abilities. Sylvester Stallone, for example, wrote and starred in his hit, *Rocky*. "Bobby is like Sylvester Stallone with more hair." Now you're talking!

Remember to keep personal taste out of the equation…consider first, the box office success! This is an industry FIRST.

The Act of Becoming is Doing.

It is not wishing. It is not resenting. It is facing fears and *naysayers*. It is rising up every morning and performing the tasks that build character and ability; actions that enable you to do more than you ever dreamed possible. And it all starts by making two decisions: the decision to get started, and the decision to NEVER quit!

So how do you know where and how to get started?

The first and most important rule in getting started is: **Take Nothing Personally.**

More often than not, the best medicine is the hardest to take. When you open your mind to information as simply *information* it is nothing personal or derogatory. You will hear, understand and respond to things you were never before able to accept.

Remember, it is not about you.
It is about the craft, the work, and the results.

The second most important rule is: **find a good coach.**

Put your ear to the ground and take notes on what you hear. Actors are generally a gabby bunch who love to gossip. Take advantage of this trait!

Ask around. *But ask the Right Questions!*

I believe most people get hung up on their search because they are often asking the wrong questions, or are expecting the wrong answers, and consequently, they pick the wrong coach. They quickly become disappointed in their selection and finally conclude they were right all along, convinced that they don't really need a coach.

Several examples of the wrong questions might be:

1. Will this coach make me famous?
2. Will your coach do for me what they have done for you?
3. I work only one way. Will this coach teach that way?

We all love to talk about what we are doing and who we are doing it with. Keep this in mind when it comes to finding a coach. Simply ask, "Who are you studying with?" The answers people give are usually very honest, and the candid answers often include facts as well as feelings about their coach.

So start right where you are. Ask the right people, those who have qualities you admire, the right questions.

Here are some examples of good questions:

1. Who are you studying with? (Even better: With whom are you studying?)
2. What are you reading? Can you recommend a good book?
3. What method or style do you study?
4. What other opportunities are out there that I could take advantage of in order to better learn the craft?

By asking these types of questions, these working actors will be more than glad to offer their advice. Just keep in mind that a lot of advice is as *useless* as it is *useful*. Take notes and review them later where you can be more objective. If the same information keeps coming up in different conversations, it will generally be more valuable than just one person's opinion.

Working actors have a body of work on stage and/or on-camera from which they can share openly about what they have experienced or learned. Simply stated, they speak from experience, not from conjecture or rumor.

Be wary of those individuals who share opinions that have no credence or value other than it being their own feeling or personal bias. In fact, I was one of those very people early in my career.

Having worked hard for a number of years to establish myself as a reputable, dependable and valuable actor in the theatre, I bad-mouthed actors who were commercial or those who considered film-style acting an art form. *"HA!"* I would say loudly and ignorantly, *"if they don't get it right, they just do it again! Where is the skill and discipline in that?"*

As I got to know the actors who were earning hundreds of dollars per day, whom I considered *less than talented*, I began to think, *"If it is so easy, I could do the commercial work in the day and theatre at night."*

My first audition was a disaster. Using all of my skills to project and to emote, I had the auditors plastered to the back wall while I wailed and emoted without regard to the intimate space. I was dismissed with the usual kind but clear nod of *Thank you*. Proud of the power and strength that I used, I strutted from the room only to see every actor in the green room staring at me like I had a third eye. "Hmmm," I thought. "I even got their attention!"

It took several trusted, talented friends and acquaintances to suggest the same coach who was training actors for the camera, before I finally allowed myself to face the truth. The truth was, I knew nothing about how to perform for a camera and I would have to humble myself to start from what felt like scratch and develop many new skills.

Soon, I was introduced to the unknown and un-explored territory of acting for the camera. All of my years on stage did not prepare me for the steady, unblinking eye of the camera. That eye sees all thought, action and intention with a clarity and definition that only the first row of an audience might see at a live performance in one of those intimate spaces where you are practically sitting on the stage. Then, with even more discernment than a human being has...**the camera never blinks.**

Strange, disconcerting things began to happen. My left became my right. Every direction was for the camera or the monitor, not for me, the actor. The lights were hotter, closer. My scene partners were standing on my feet, I could smell their shampoo and what brand of toothpaste they used (or didn't). I was assaulted with light meters and measuring tape. Directions were more about what I had to do to make it look good for camera. Claustrophobia set in like a fog; thick, blinding and ready to suffocate. I was a stranger in a strange land.

Perhaps that's how you feel now; uncertain whether acting for the camera is for you or not. I will assure you that if you must act, you already know the answer. You will do whatever it takes at whatever the cost. By never giving up, you will succeed.

At the peak of my commercial, industrial and spokesman opportunities, students who were in my category would ask, "Why would we train with you when you are going out for the same jobs we are?" "*Simple,*" I would reply, "*You are uniquely you and I am uniquely me. I am not right for every client even though I may be perfect for the job. How or what I say, may not be what the client was thinking I would do; yet what you do may be exactly what the client was hoping for.*" Uniquity!

CHAPTER THREE

CHARACTERISTICS OF A WORKING ACTOR

A working actor takes the challenge of juggling schedules with as much agility as the juggler who is able to keep many balls in the air at one time. The secret is to handle one ball at a time, while keeping your peripheral vision on the others. A working actor is *Dependable*, *Reliable*, and *Available*. She has a professional agent who is aware of her present and growing capabilities based on the work that is always presented her.

> Working actors are too busy to badmouth others. They know that the person they badmouth today may be the someone who could give them a job tomorrow. Working Actors are Dependable, Reliable, and Available.

Actors who have a *"real job"* or *"the 'ol nine to fiver,"* spend the majority of their time working for someone else's dream.

A professional actor is someone who is always working. It is not always for pay. It is more often doing self-promotion. Professional actors are busy sending out their headshots, resumes and demo reels to leads they have found on the Internet or in the local production guide. They are schmoozing at industry gatherings, parties and functions. Professional actors are continuously reading, taking classes and researching films and plays. They know these are valuable tools that better prepare them for their next professional job.

THEATRE IS THE FOUNDATION

Most people who are serious about acting are found in the theatre, spending every free moment away from their *nine to fiver* there. I know of no better way to spend this time. The theatre is your foundation. It develops a tough, roguish ability to adapt to almost any situation at any given time. It explores and develops a person's ability to adapt, to accept change, and it humbles the most rigid of characters. Perhaps the greatest reward is the instant gauge for your ingenuity, ability and success as well as for your mistakes.

The time demand is enormous and the financial reward is usually less than wonderful. When I see a terrible theatrical performance, I still appreciate the hard work and deep love of the craft that went into making that flop.

When you decide you want to join the business of acting for the camera, you must be available 24/7, and usually on a less-than-24-hour notice.

Theatre is the perfect place to pursue the invaluable practice of getting to know professionals. If you don't know anyone who is working in production full time, it is not hard to start your search. Here are a few different ways to begin.

ATTEND THE THEATRE REGULARLY

Fill your weekend calendar with theatre events. Attend as many of the local events as possible, keeping your program from each show, and make notes on the performers who most impressed you with their presence and abilities. Your program is a valuable resource of names and information. You may discover the props mistress' name appears in a number of programs, propping numerous shows. Same for the lighting tech, sound, wardrobe, etc. "WAIT A MINUTE!" You say, "What the heck does a costumer have to do with my getting to know actors, and where those actors study or what they know?"

Like I said before, we (especially we in this business) love to gossip. Ask the *behind the scenes* techies or support artists, and they will tell you everything you ever wanted to know and more. It will be up to you to *filter* the information that you receive. Filtering the information is what I will talk about later as being an exercise in listening, the first and most important step in acting.

> Listening and filtering what people say about others
> is hearing what they don't say.

What others *don't say* is often more telling than what they *do say*. This is especially true for those who have learned the value of not saying anything negative about those who are in the same business. Remember what I said about gossip.

A second way to get started finding out about those you wish to know better, is to do what you are doing right now. READ! Autobiographies and biographies of actors, producers, and people in the industry are wonderfully rich in what they did to attain their fame and achieve their goals.

GET IN A WORKSHOP NOW

You will want to get started in an on-going workshop as soon as possible. You will not learn acting by osmosis, nor will your talents and abilities that served you at the age of 10 serve you well at the age of 20 or 30 or beyond.

> You can't afford it? You can't afford not to. If you consider your training an expense, you will neither choose to learn, nor will you choose to benefit. Training is an investment!

There is not an agent or an acting coach anywhere that owes you anything. You are investing in your future. You are investing in yourself, so choose wisely whose and what type of workshop you are going to attend.

By being enrolled in a reputable and widely recognized workshop, you are far more valuable in the marketplace. You will be much more quickly recognized by agents. Too many aspiring actors do it in reverse. Without any training or knowledge, they approach an agent, hoping to get signed. When the phone doesn't ring for six months they blame the agent for not sending them out on all of the auditions they have been hearing about. Be a wise investor. Save everyone's time and resources by enrolling in a reputable workshop now.

Acting in film is learned best by working with a coach who is familiar with the camera and how the camera is used to emphasize your work. Your workshops should include working in front of the camera as well as the opportunity to learn what goes on behind the camera.

AUDIT FIRST

The coach should provide an open audit. The opportunity to attend a workshop session without cost or obligation will give you a first-hand awareness of the dynamics, the feel and the instruction that is provided. The decision you will be making should be one that is considered a long-term commitment.

It is important that no matter what you heard about the workshop or the coach who runs it, YOU are the one who is going to be investing your time and resources in the work. If you do not hit it off with or feel good about the coach, the group or any other aspect of the workshop, keep shopping. Your goal is to find a workshop in which you will feel encouraged to grow.

Don't get me wrong. I am not suggesting that every little thing is going to click right away. You should be challenged. There may be a good deal of information that goes right over your head. You can expect some exercises and assignments that you won't understand. There will be some that you may have heard many times already.

Be sure to judge and consider the intention as well as the directions given. A good coach will see the problems as well as strengths and accomplishments that the actor can't or won't see.

I feel strongly that an acting workshop is not a science or mathematics course in which the answers and formulas are finite or the results entirely predictable. Each student or participant should feel challenged to develop his own unique style while using time-tested and proven techniques and methods as guides.

If you are lucky, you may find a great workshop that offers a three-month initial commitment, and then allows a month-to-month relationship. Most workshops, however, require a minimum commitment of one year.

Keep in mind that acting is a profession like any other. There are those doing only the minimum, and there are those who are taking charge of their future by working every day to be the best at what they choose to do. Which are you?

If you are looking for a challenge that will provide you with an opportunity to work every day, you have found it. Examine in depth the process of *Listen, Feel and Respond*. It is the process of learning to listen to your heart, your intuition and your creative spirit.

SUMMARY OF PART ONE

Like so many actors, most know they want to act, they even feel they know how. But taking the leap into workshops, seminars, classes, showcases, securing an agent and so on is as frightening as being stuck on a merry-go-round that is going too fast. It is merry until the speed becomes too great and the force pulls you outward and throws you off.

The most important thing, no matter how good you are as an actor, is contacts. As the new actor in town, you will need to start a *buzz* about yourself. Creating allies and relationships with coaches, casting directors, agents, managers, producers, directors and earning the admiration of peers are absolutely essential in finding your success. This is a team effort. No one does it alone.

The next section of this book, **Part Two**, is best read in bite-sized pieces. The *Listen, Feel, Respond* method of preparation and delivery is one that is recognized by almost every person who has ever dabbled with acting, and may write off the details as either too lengthy, or too simple.

I have students who professed they were listening effectively. To their dismay they discovered, in following the exercises included in this book, that they had barely scratched the surface. So, keep an open mind and a willing spirit.

Part Two

The 3-step process of Listen, Feel, Respond.

"Repetition is the Mother of Perfection."

Like the detailed process we went through when learning to drive, each step seems at times lengthy, repetitive or even frightening. Every detail required our full and complete attention. And, no matter how difficult the lessons, our desire to drive was stronger than our fear not to.

Mastering *Listen Feel Respond* is no different. What requires repetitive study and application will soon yield almost mindless ease of understanding and operation.

Remember when you were given the keys to the driver's ed. car and you knew you were going to drive out of the lot and onto the public street for the first time? It was like slow motion ... the very act of where to put the key into the ignition slot required concentrated effort. Paying attention to every detail, you adjusted the mirrors and the seat, and noticed how the wheel felt in your hands.

Remember the uncertainty of when, exactly, the car would respond to the pressure of your foot on the accelerator pedal? Remember the first response of the brakes? Discovering the need to apply more gas uphill and less downhill, and a plethora of other small but significant actions that were new and unexpected was thrilling.

Think now about the last time you drove: do you even remember putting the key in the ignition? Or how you even got to where you were going? All the required steps and operations were automatic...or mindless.

It isn't that you didn't give each operation thought, or that you didn't have to pay attention, but the act of repetition allowed for the relaxed and natural performance of each individual action in getting you to and from your destination safely and successfully.

Taking the time and energy to focus on each step of the *Listen Feel Respond* process, you will once again experience the frustration of repeated difficulties and failures. Nevertheless, continued efforts and focused attention will most certainly, yield rewarding and positive results.

Let's get started.

CHAPTER FOUR

Step One:
LISTEN

Listening is a skill that you will develop and improve upon for the rest of your life. Listening is the first and the most misunderstood step in the three-step process of acting.

Listening is, by nature and by habit, selective. People who are unable to select and process what they hear are sometimes labeled autistic. Too much information can be overwhelming, confusing and detrimental in extremes and yet too little information is frustrating, limiting and also detrimental.

I attended the 2004 Denver International Film Festival opening, hosting Jamie Foxx in the leading role of Mr. Ray Charles (Robinson) opposite Kerry Washington as his wife, Bea, in the new release of *RAY*. In that movie there is what I consider to be the perfect scene, where Ray explains to Bea how he is able to *Hear* the way she *Sees*. The performance that follows is such a great depiction of how a well-written script, depicted by powerful images, strong direction and carefully constructed production values, allows us to better understand how much of what can be heard is completely ignored.

So the question is: What, as actors, are we supposed to listen to?

LISTENING—A TOOL FOR PREPARATION AND DECISION MAKING

Listening is a tool that is developed to aide you in decision-making. It starts when you enter the building for an audition. Perhaps it is obvious that as the door closes behind you, it shuts off the sound of the street, the traffic and the noise that is part of most city streets.

What may not be so obvious is what you hear if you are running late or if you are having difficulty in locating the stairs or elevator or hallway that will lead you to the audition.

> Frustration is a confusing and hungry noise that eats away at confidence and preparedness.

When you finally discover the door to the office where your audition is to be held, you may realize you have been listening to too much of the wrong stuff. Now, you begin over-compensating with excuses. "I couldn't find this place, I had bad directions..." The secretary at the desk, who is signing you in, is smiling his protective smile and hiding his true feelings about how negative and blaming you are, and replies with a simple, "I'm sorry you had a difficult time." and suggests you sign in.

Maybe just by reading this, you are able to re-live a time when you have done this very thing. The feeling of urgency and panic, of frustration and regret are fresh and re-awakened. The *noise* of those feelings, the *noise* of that situation was so loud that you may not have been able to do as well as if you had studied your map ahead of time.

> We have so much more responsibility to prepare ourselves for success than we do to prepare ourselves for failure.

When you are unsure of the neighborhood or directions, prepare yourself by driving to the location the day before. You will know how much time it will take to get there on the day of the audition. Going that extra distance to prepare for the unseen is a way in which we filter out the noise that will distract us from hearing positive, supportive sounds.

What you were listening to in the scenario I just described was a noise that will continue to ring in your ears, well into your audition. It will impact your read in ways you may not even be consciously aware. This then, leads me to the point that *Listening* is not just performed with your ears.

> *Listening* is an exercise that is best performed with tools that require an open, relaxed and sensitive heart, mind and soul.

Here is a listening exercise:

SEE what you *HEAR*

In a classroom full of people, select two people. The first should be a person that you may know, or is someone you have made a close and personal connection with. I will refer to this person as *LISTENER*. The second is to be someone who will observe. I will refer to them as the *OBSERVER*.

Remind the entire room that this is a listening exercise and that you trust all who wish to participate will follow the rules exactly.

Ask everyone but the Observer to close their eyes and keep them closed. Now, only the observer and you have your eyes open.

Look directly at the Listener and say a true and heart-felt message to this person. It may be something like, "Caron, you have the most beautiful eyes and you are always doing something positive for others." Whatever the statement, it must be one that is true and will resonate with truth.

Immediately following your statement, roll your eyes or in some physical way, show that what you just said is being refuted as a lie. Only your Observer will see the after-statement gesture.

Then ask everyone to open their eyes.

Ask the Listener what she heard.

Then ask the Observer what he heard.

A class discussion should follow, pointing out several things:

First, that both the Listener and the Observer heard the same thing, but that the Listener was denied the whole truth by being denied one of her senses. Secondly, that listening with just our ears is not listening fully, and that more often than not listening with just our ears is a way in which we are lying to ourselves. We are choosing not to hear the whole truth, or to hear only what we want to hear.

Remember the old statement, "your actions are so loud, I can't hear what you're saying."

> Now, I hope that you are beginning to understand that
> Listening involves more than what we hear with our ears.

Recognizing that listening is as much a part of what you *see* as it is with what you *hear* is not only enlightening, it is liberating.

Go one step further. Imagine *listening* for what you can't *hear* and to what you can't *see*.

Here's another *listening* exercise.

Pair up everyone in the room with the person they know the least.

Assuming everyone is physically able to sit on the floor for at least 30 minutes, ask the paired *strangers* to sit on the floor with their backs supporting each other, back to back.

Suggest they rest the back of their heads on the back of their partner's heads. Get as much physical contact back-to-back as comfortably possible.

An added benefit of this is discovering who has problems with sharing their personal space, a problem that must be dealt with for on-camera development.

Each person will have five minutes to share a story about when they first fell in love.

After the stories have been shared, ask the partners to face each other and have the person who listened to the story repeat it back to the story teller.

After both have repeated the story back, lead a discussion on what they FELT from the other person's body as they listened as well as when they spoke. What were the actions, what were the reactions?

Listening has to do with how you move.

Listening is affected by our body language or body functions, heart rate, temperature, nervousness, calm and so on. Our spirit or our heart can translate what we are hearing in ways our ears or our eyes are unable.

It is important to recognize that the camera is able to pick up these subtle and often overlooked reactions of the heart. That is how and why it is essential to study your craft in front of a camera, in a workshop where the replay is as important as the work itself.

I want to inspire your own thoughts and your own ideas as to how many ways you can begin to develop your own listening skills. The idea is to START thinking and listening outside of the proverbial box.

With that in mind, take a minute to try this simple exercise. You must connect **ALL nine dots** (three rows of three dots forming a square of nine dots) with **only 4 straight lines and without lifting your pencil from the page.**

Go ahead. Try it. I will provide the answer at the end of chapter 16. Here's the puzzle of dots.

```
.   .   .

.   .   .

.   .   .
```

Okay, so you get the fact that listening deals with much more than what is pounding against your eardrum. Before we go further, allow me to explain the overall process and purpose of *Listen, Feel, Respond*.

BEING "OPEN" IS BEING NON-JUDGMENTAL

Developing and strengthening the skill to be *open* is your greatest asset in any delivery. It is the active choice to be open to whatever you can and whatever you will allow to affect you.

Here are just a few of the subjects that affect most of us very strongly. In fact, our nations defend or kill for these very things:

*Bigotry *Racism *Capitalism *Communism *Religion
*Sexism *Politics *Land

You will receive strong, heartfelt emotion from anyone with whom you start a conversation on any of these topics. Stories and firsthand experiences to back their every word, to emphasize their point, will accompany the expression and attitude with which the storytellers deliver their message.

The exercise or idea is not to start a fight, but to OBSERVE how simple subjects like those listed above, have a complex and heartfelt effect on the human condition. It is your job as an actor to be OBSERVANT. Then, having observed, be able to replicate what you have observed in different settings and situations that will allow for and create equally strong reactions.

Making decisions on HOW a line is to be read (or delivered)
before you examine WHY that line was written
is artistic and performance suicide.

Try this simple exercise. Read the next line to yourself.
I hate you.
You have already formulated and prepared your read of that line by now, so go ahead. Say it out loud ...with meaning!

"I HATE YOU!"
Emphasize it!
"I **HATE** YOU!"
More!
"I HATE YOU!"

As soon as your blood pressure comes back down and your face returns to its normal color, and your racing heart begins to slow back to its acceptable pace, prepare to read the next line.

HOW you read that line was indeed, powerful and effective. However, it was also predictable and, whether you want to admit it or not, is how the majority of actors will deliver it at their cold read.

The *WHY* of the Line.

First, ask *WHY* you would be asked to say the line. *WHY* do you hate the person to whom you are saying, *I hate you*?

WHAT has this person done to you? *WHEN* did it occur? *WHO* did the deed? *WHERE* were you when it was said or done? *WHY* do you think that person did what he or she did?

Using this scenario, imagine how you might say *I hate you* differently from the way you formed it the first time:

The *What* (the person did) is unspeakable and shocking.
The *When* was unexpected and recent.
The *Who* is unquestionably trusted and deeply loved.
The *Where* is a public, open location.
The *Why* was purposeful spite.

Now, you have this person right in front of you. (If this is a camera audition, the person is the camera lens) You are given the cue, "Action." This person whom you love, trust and have never questioned, reveals the heinous deed crushing your every expectation and desire for this relationship beyond repair. With unexpected, undeniable and unavoidable force you respond:

(Hurt, tearing up, barely able to speak)…*I hate you*.

The *INTENTION* is created by what you *HEAR*. What you *HEAR* is SELECTIVE. So if you are not working on how many different ways you can *LISTEN*, you are limiting yourself only to the predictable means to which you have become accustomed.

Listening is as active as it is responsive. So, naturally, this leads to the next step in the three-step process of *Listen, Feel, Respond*.

CHAPTER FIVE

Step Two:
FEEL

Is it possible to know how you FEEL without first REACTING? "Well, duh! What kind of a stupid question is that?" You may ask. But I challenge you to ask yourself, as easy as that task may sound in life, how easy is it when we have a script in front of us?

ONE QUESTION TO NEVER ASK

Have you ever asked your director "How do I say this line?" Oh, how I cringe when I hear that. I suppose, in a pinch, that kind of shorthand question requiring a shorthand answer may be appropriate, but **you will never hear that question coming from an actor who has done her homework, research and preparation.** Certainly not from an actor who allows herself to be in the moment ...to be exercising her ability to listen effectively!

The second step in the three-step process is simply, FEELING.
Ready for another exercise?

AN EXERCISE ON FEELING

First, take a moment to close your eyes and breathe deep. Do it now. Good. Now read, then follow the directions in the next paragraph carefully.

1.) Go outdoors or to a room in which you spend the least amount of time, and just be still.

2.) Listen to the new setting. What do you hear?

3.) Ask yourself how you FEEL.

A)   Is this new setting more relaxing?

B)   Uncomfortable?

C)   Calming?

D)   Stressful?

4.) Label and note whatever feelings come to mind. Study where they register or where they are felt.

A)   Your solar plexus?

B)   Your face?

C)   Your pelvis?

Where and *What* are the questions to focus on.

Okay, now you are back.

Hopefully you were able to experience a different feeling than what you had while you were here reading, just a few minutes ago.

> Did you find that what you felt, or started to feel, was less of a thought and more of an action?
> Did your heart rate (an action) speed up or slow down?
> Perhaps your breathing (action) was deeper, slower, shallower or faster?

The discipline of allowing and expressing our feelings openly and honestly is a discipline that is often put aside so as to protect and serve the public expectation of normality in human behavior.

Consider how you respond to a loved one's request like the following, made in the privacy of your home versus in a crowded mall:

"Tell me you love me." Or: "Don't tell me to shut up. You shut up!"

We have learned to hide our true feelings based on the expectations of our surroundings. That is a normal and intelligent thing to do in most cases. However, revealing the feelings that most all of us feel, but choose not to share openly, is precisely where actors have their greatest successes.

Comedians take that simple idea or story or life experience that so many of us have encountered and simply add what we really want to say or to respond to, and out of discovery, we laugh at the simple truth!

> Allowing truth removes doubt. Denial of truth takes a lot of practice and huge amounts of energy.

Compare the ease with which a child takes on the task of allowing imagination to create environment, relationships and storylines. They have little or no fear when they are pretending. They use what they have observed (heard) and are doing what they were made to feel. Because the child is simple, so is the character the child creates. It is all about trust and commitment.

TRUST that you will be present as the character that you have prepared, and COMMIT to the moment-to-moment discoveries in what you *hear*.

What is difficult for us as adults is letting go of expectation, judgment and fear.

Facing the truth of our feelings will redefine our ability as actors. It will allow for discoveries that we could not otherwise plan. It will indeed, create a trusting and honest performance that will be shared by the viewers because you will be sharing the moment right along with them.

Here's a little ditty that has been circulating on the web. Perhaps you are one of the many who have received it, but this time, I want you to read it as though it is a short subject film in which you have been asked to be the taxi driver.

THE CAB RIDE

Twenty years ago, I drove a cab for a living.

When I arrived at 2:30 a.m. the building was dark except for a single light in a ground floor window. Under these circumstances, many drivers would just honk once or twice, wait a minute, and then drive away. But, I had seen too many impoverished people who depended on taxis as their only means of transportation. Unless a situation smelled of danger, I always went to the door. This passenger might be someone who needs my assistance, I reasoned to myself.

So I walked to the door and knocked.

"Just a minute," answered a frail, elderly voice.

I could hear something being dragged across the floor.

After a long pause, the door opened. A small woman in her 80's stood before me. She was wearing a print dress and a pillbox hat with a veil pinned on it, like somebody out of a 1940s movie. By her side was a small nylon suitcase.

The apartment looked as if no one had lived in it for years. All the furniture was covered with sheets. There were no clocks on the walls, no knickknacks or utensils on the counters. In the corner was a cardboard box filled with photos and glassware.

"Would you carry my bag out to the car?" she said.
I took the suitcase to the cab, and then returned to assist the woman.
She took my arm and we walked slowly toward the curb.
She kept thanking me for my kindness.
"It's nothing," I told her. "I just try to treat my passengers the way I would want my mother treated."
"Oh, you're such a good boy," she said.

When we got in the cab, she gave me an address, and then asked, "Could you drive through downtown?"
"It's not the shortest way," I answered quickly.
"Oh, I don't mind," she said. "I'm in no hurry. I'm on my way to a hospice."
I looked in the rear-view mirror. Her eyes were glistening.
"I don't have any family left," she continued. "The doctor says I don't have very long."

I quietly reached over and shut off the meter.
"What route would you like me to take?" I asked.

For the next two hours, we drove through the city. She showed me the building where she had once worked as an elevator operator.
We drove through the neighborhood where she and her husband had lived when they were newlyweds. She had me pull up in front of a furniture warehouse that had once been a ballroom where she had gone dancing as a girl.

Sometimes she'd ask me to slow in front of a particular building or corner and would sit staring into the darkness, saying nothing.

As the first hint of sun was creasing the horizon, she suddenly said,
"I'm tired. Let's go now."
We drove in silence to the address she had given me.
It was a low building, like a small convalescent home, with a driveway
that passed under a portico.

Two orderlies came out to the cab as soon as we pulled up.
They were solicitous and intent, watching her every move. They must
have been expecting her.
I opened the trunk and took the small suitcase to the door.
The woman was already seated in a wheelchair.

"How much do I owe you?" she asked, reaching into her purse.
"Nothing," I said.
"You have to make a living," she answered.
"There are other passengers," I responded.

Almost without thinking, I bent and gave her a hug. She held onto me
tightly.
"You gave an old woman a little moment of joy," she said.
"Thank you."
I squeezed her hand, and then walked into the dim morning light.
Behind me, a door shut. It was the sound of the closing of a life.

What do you *feel*? Is it a sense of ownership? Is it as though you remember
having lived the story? What did you *Hear*? What senses did you *hear* with?

START THINKING CINEMA-GRAPHICALLY

Images have tremendous impact on how and what we *feel*.

Go back within the story and review what, specifically, you connected with. Take the story apart image by image. As you story board the images, you begin to pay particular attention to details that would otherwise be left out.

1. How do you construct the story in terms of images and how do you, as a character in the story, fit into these images?
2. What images are close-up and which are wide?
3. Can you hear what Foley effects you would add to highlight and strengthen sounds that would ordinarily be passed over? i.e., their footsteps on the walk as they approached the cab, etc.

Add to the images as many of your other senses as possible and you secure the image and feeling that much deeper or stronger!

Let your imagination reawaken the memories of actual places you have been. Allow the feelings associated with those places to surface, then copy and paste them into the written story.

Spend some time exploring these images that you are creating and allow yourself to experience how your feelings change as your images change. Design more or less visual changes to the background. Add palm trees, or deciduous trees. Explore. Create. Imagine and allow whatever you choose, and study how those image choices connect deeply with what you feel.

> Images that stimulate emotion will be recorded deeply into your memory and enable you to recall and feel the same emotion for the rest of your life.

Allow as many senses as possible to be activated by what you hear.

1. While stepping out of the cab into the early morning, did you smell anything?
2. If it just rained, can you smell the ozone?
3. With the moist air, is it carrying any faint odor of garbage in the alleyway?

Ask yourself questions like these all the way through the piece as each location appears.

DETAILS

Did you *hear* the sweep of the big front door as the old woman steps out? Are the hinges over-oiled, so that you can even smell it dripping down the seams of the hinge into the doorjamb?

Every detail evokes a distinct feeling, called up from memory, or created anew through discovery. This, in turn, produces new feelings. This process of details inspiring feelings and those feelings providing more details, enriches and enhances your performance and response.

In short, everything you hear elicits a specific emotion or *feeling*.

As you develop your awareness of details,
you are creating more emotional choices
and *Feelings* that affect your responses.

If you are stuck on words to describe how you feel, after completing this next exercise, you might as well throw that excuse out the window!

FEELINGS EXERCISE

In the list of Feelings below, I have left room on both sides of each feeling for you to create a sentence using each feeling. The main headings like *afraid, eager* and *interested,* are commonly-used words. I want you to write sentences using the more descriptive, less familiar words listed under each heading. By using the feeling in a sentence, you will better associate its use and meaning, enabling you to recall the flavor, emotion and sound it can produce when you need it. Please make your sentences in the first person. (Make it about you.)

EXAMPLE: *I was*   appalled   *by his lack of judgment.*

AFRAID

1._____aghast_____.

2._____alarmed_____.

3._____anxious_____.

4._____appalled_____.

5._____apprehensive_____.

6._____awed_____.

7._____breathless_____.

8._____chicken_____.

9._____cold_____.

10._____cowardly_____.

11._____diffident_____.

12._____dismayed_____.

13._____doubtful_____.

14._____fainthearted_____.

15._____fearful_____.

16._____fidgety_____.

17._____frightened_____.

18._____hesitant_____.

19._____horrified_____.

20._____hysterical_____.

21._____immobilized_____.

22._____insecure_____.

23._____irresolute_____.

24._____menaced_____.

25._____nervous_____.

26._____panicky_____.

27._____paralyzed_____.

28._____petrified_____.

29._____restless_____.

30._____scared_____.

31._____shaky_____.

32._____shocked_____.

33._____suspicious_____.

34._____terrified_____.

35._____threatened_____.

36._____timid_____.

37._____timorous_____.

38._____tremulous_____.

39._____trembly_____.

40._____worried_____.

41._____yellow_____.

ANGRY

1._____acrimonious_____.

2._____annoyed_____.

3._____belligerent_____.

4._____bitter_____.

5._____boiling_____.

6._____contemptuous_____.

7._____cross_____.

8._____defiant_____.

9._____enraged_____.

10._____fuming_____.

11._____furious_____.

12._____in a stew_____.

13._____incensed_____.

14._____indignant_____.

15._____inflamed_____.

16._____infuriated_____.

17._____irate_____.

18._____irritated_____.

19._____offended_____.

20._____piqued_____.

21._____provoked_____.

22._____resentful_____.

23._____sulky_____.

24._____sullen_____.

25._____up in arms_____.

26._____virulent_____.

27._____worked up_____.

28._____wrathful_____.

29._____wrought up_____.

DOUBTFUL

1._____cautious_____.

2._____distant_____.

3._____distrustful_____.

4._____dubious_____.

5._____hesitant_____.

6._____indecisive_____.

7._____perplexed_____.

8._____questioning_____.

9._____skeptical_____.

10._____suspicious_____.

11._____unbelieving_____.

12._____uncertain_____.

13._____wavering_____.

EAGER

1._____anxious_____.

2._____ardent_____.

3._____avid_____.

4._____desirous_____.

5._____earnest_____.

6._____fervent_____.

7._____fervid_____.

8._____intent_____.

9._____itchy_____.

10._____keen_____.

11._____zealous_____.

FEARLESS

1._____audacious_____.

2._____bold_____.

3._____brave_____.

4._____calm_____.

5._____certain_____.

6._____confident_____.

7._____courageous_____.

8._____daring_____.

9._____dauntless_____.

10._____determined_____.

11._____firm_____.

12._____gallant_____.

13._____hardy_____.

14._____heroic_____.

15._____independent_____.

16._____resolute_____.

17._____secure_____.

18._____self-reliant_____.

19._____strong_____.

HAPPY

1._____airy_____.

2._____animated_____.

3._____blissful_____.

4._____blithe_____.

5._____bright_____.

6._____brisk_____.

7._____buoyant_____.

8._____cheerful_____.

9._____cheery_____.

10._____comfortable_____.

11._____contented_____.

12._____convivial_____.

13._____debonair_____.

14._____ecstatic_____.

15._____elated_____.

16._____enthusiastic_____.

17._____exhilarated_____.

18._____exultant_____.

19._____festive_____.

20._____frisky_____.

21._____gay_____.

22._____genial_____.

23._____giddy_____.

24._____glad_____.

25._____gleeful_____.

26._____grateful_____.

27._____high-spirited_____.

28._____hilarious_____.

29._____inspired_____.

30._____jaunty_____.

31._____jocular_____.

32._____jolly_____.

33._____jovial_____.

34._____joyous_____.

35._____jubilant_____.

36._____lighthearted_____.

37._____lively_____.

38._____merry_____.

39._____mirthful_____.

40._____peaceful_____.

41._____playful_____.

42._____pleased_____.

43._____rapturous_____.

44._____satisfied_____.

45._____saucy_____.

46._____serene_____.

47._____silly_____.

48._____sparkling_____.

49._____sprightly_____.

50._____spirited_____.

51._____sunny_____.

52._____thankful_____.

53._____tranquil_____.

54._____vivacious_____.

55._____warm_____.

HURT

1._____aching_____.

2._____afflicted_____.

3._____agonized_____.

4._____crushed_____.

5._____despairing_____.

6._____distressed_____.

7._____dolorous_____.

8._____embarrassed_____.

9._____grieved_____.

10._____hapless_____.

11._____heartbroken_____.

12._____injured_____.

13._____mournful_____.

14._____offended_____.

15._____pained_____.

16._____pathetic_____.

17._____piteous_____.

18._____rueful_____.

19._____shamed_____.

20._____tortured_____.

21._____tragic_____.

22._____victimized_____.

23._____woeful_____.

24._____worried_____.

INTERESTED

1._____absorbed_____.

2._____affected_____.

3._____concerned_____.

4._____curious_____.

5._____engrossed_____.

6._____excited_____.

7._____fascinated_____.

8._____inquisitive_____.

9._____intrigued_____.

10._____nosey_____.

11._____snoopy_____.

SAD

1._____cheerless_____.

2._____choked up_____.

3._____clouded_____.

4._____crestfallen_____.

5._____dark_____.

6._____dejected_____.

7._____depressed_____.

8._____despondent_____.

9._____disconsolate_____.

10._____discontented_____.

11._____discouraged_____.

12._____disheartened_____.

13._____dismal_____.

14._____downhearted_____.

15._____downcast_____.

16._____dreadful_____.

17._____dreary_____.

18._____dull_____.

19._____empty_____.

20._____flat_____.

21._____funereal_____.

22._____gloomy_____.

23._____glum_____.

24._____grief-stricken_____.

25._____hollow_____.

26._____joyless_____.

27._____melancholy_____.

28._____moody_____.

29._____moping_____.

30._____mournful_____.

31._____mumpish_____.

32._____oppressed_____.

33._____out of sorts_____.

34._____quiet_____.

35._____somber_____.

36._____sorrowful_____.

37._____spiritless_____.

38._____sulky_____.

39._____sullen_____.

40._____sympathetic_____.

41._____unhappy_____.

42._____vacant_____.

43._____woebegone_____.

44._____woeful_____.

_____(YOU LABEL)

1._____affectionate_____.

2._____awkward_____.

3._____bewildered_____.

4._____bushed_____.

5._____dependant_____.

6._____encouraged_____.

7._____envious_____.

8._____jealous_____.

9._____loving_____.

10._____nauseated_____.

11._____powerless_____.

12._____proud_____.

13._____reassured_____.

14._____respectful_____.

15._____seductive_____.

16._____sexy_____.

17._____soft_____.

18._____submissive_____.

19._____surprised_____.

20._____sweaty_____.

21._____talkative_____.

22._____tolerant_____.

If you were able to complete the exercise of using each feeling word in a sentence, keeping it first person, you may have discovered that you now have a tremendous storehouse of feelings descriptions. This storehouse will become very useful as you continue to develop your *Listen, Feel, Respond* abilities. Surprisingly, you will have answers to the age-old question, "How do you feel?"

This enormous list of feelings may also come in very handy whenever you prepare and develop characters for your current and future roles.

We have discussed the first two elements that create an honest and effective performance, but now it is time to let the viewer see what you have been working on. The third and final step is to *Respond*.

CHAPTER SIX

Step Three:
RESPOND

Defining the Problem

The *response* one gives in a performance is too often based on what the actor had planned ahead of time. That is, the actor chooses to play the *attitude*.

The most appropriate and effective response is based mainly, if not entirely, on what is *heard* or on **how** what is *heard,* creates *feelings* that should be used.

If the actor is not really *listening* and/or paying attention to what is referred to as the *beats,* or is *in the moment,* or as in my examples, has simply and honestly allowed a *feeling* from what he *heard,* the actor will blurt out his line without regard to how it should be delivered.

The response or the delivered line will be too early, too late, *flat* or worst of all, detached.

Have you ever been directed to "Pick up the pace! We don't want to lose our audience!" You immediately begin to speak faster and step on your scene partners' lines. The energy of the scene becomes more frenetic and perhaps even louder. You are doing your best to follow the direction you were given, working hard to satisfy the director.

It's true, the audience will be applauding the end of the play sooner, but it will not be for any of the great performances. Okay, I am sure that it has never really been *that* bad, but you get the idea. What happened was with the best of intent, but with a lack of understanding for the whole picture.

Another example:

You have studied your script, you are fully aware of the setting; you know the storyline from it's beginning through its end. You understand the characters, who they are, what they want and need from each other, and therefore you know the conflict and how it is to be resolved. You are prepared to read the scene.

Having made the decisions and agreed on those decisions with your partner and director, you start in, prepared to deliver your lines as you planned. Then, something happens that you had not planned and you are thrown from responding as you had anticipated.

Offering a Solution

The actor who can receive the direction to "pick up the pace," using *Listen, Feel, Respond,* is able to generate whatever action, response or *moment* that was missing, thereby giving the *illusion* that the pace was too slow or that the audience would be lost.

Developing this self-directing ability is invaluable. It allows you to better understand and respond to the author's intent as well as that of the director.

The *Respond* portion of *Listen, Feel, Respond,* is the part that must be allowed to be the freest, or the least thought about.

Response to stimulus, whether it is with a line, an action or both, is best delivered as though it was unplanned, unrehearsed or *natural* and yet, its construction and preparation must be wholly cognitive.

I often say to my students, "actors are not paid to think, they are paid to react." That is, an actor's *thinking* takes place within the process of *preparation*; defining the character, the rehearsal process and development of everything which surrounds those decisions.

Of course, thinking is an absolute must for an actor, but let me use the following example to better illustrate my point.

In the film, *Indiana Jones and the Raiders of the Lost Ark*, actor Terry Richards was hired as an Arab Swordsman to face down the hero, Indiana Jones.

For many weeks, Mr. Richards prepared himself by working hard every day to throw the large and heavy sword this way and that to appear menacing and threatening. The day of the big scene arrived and Mr. Richards was ready. I'm sure he was thrilled to have so much on-screen time under Hollywood's great team of talent both in front of and behind the camera. The limelight was as bright as ever for him.

As cameras were brought to speed and the direction of "Action!" was called, Terry Richards went into his long, well-rehearsed swordplay to threaten Harrison Ford's character. We all know what happened at this point: film history gained another page.

Mr. Ford simply, knowingly and completely in character, pulled out his side arm and shot the armed Arabian and walked away. I will never forget the laughter that erupted in the theatre at that point. It broke all of the rules, yet it was so perfect!

I later learned that Mr. Ford made that historical decision because of abdominal pains and simply wanted to relieve himself. It is my guess that he had every intention of coming back later to get the intended shot that would include hours of coverage, showing the menacing swordplay and the lengthy battle. But a perfect solution was created when, *without thought*, and with perfect *intention* and *awareness*, Mr. Ford's character acted with a history-making action.

Equally important to recognize was the expert recognition by Mr. Richards that he take the fall!

Imagine if you will, that after so many weeks of preparation, Mr. Richards would have broken the scene by complaining, "He shot me? That's not in the script! I have worked long and hard for this scene, and he shoots me?"

Instead, with immeasurable amounts of humility and professionalism, in a split second, wherein no rehearsal or previous discussion was to clue him, he is shot at and he takes the fall! Congratulations, Mr. Richards. That was a remarkable and selfless decision that lives valiantly in film history.

Here's another example of how reacting honestly to what is heard and felt is, in its own way, just as powerful as Indy Jones and the Arabian sword fighter.

I was having a telephone conversation with one of my students regarding a scene that I had assigned him two days earlier. The scene is one where a father is helping his drug addicted daughter finish packing her bags, preparing to be taken to drug rehab. My student was asking on what line of the script the emotional transitions were to occur, commenting that he had never dealt with a child who was addicted.

"Let's go back," I suggested. "What do you, as a father, want for your child?"
"Happiness and success." He said.
"Yours or hers?" I asked.
"Hers." he replied.
"At what cost?"
"What do you mean?" He asked.
"What if her happiness and success means you have to be the bad guy, the authoritarian, the tough, unwavering and insistent father, as opposed to the demure, sensitive, weakling father who lets her have whatever she wants, whenever she wants it, because you love her?"
"Well, if you put it that way." he said, "I would prefer the former."
"Why?"
"Because I love her," he replied.

My student is better prepared now to do the scene than if he had spent hours or days working on lines and line emphasis for two simple reasons.

First, everything he chooses to actively *do* is based on his decision to love.

Secondly, he has paved the way of the scene with layers of truth that will allow him to explore the unknown relationship with the confidence of what he does know.

Finally, using the three preparatory steps of *Listen, Feel, Respond* he will be prepared to *hear* what he would not have otherwise heard. He will be enabled to *feel* and *respond* in ways that are not described or instructed on the written page.

He knows he will do whatever it takes to get his daughter packed and out the door, all because he loves her and wants the best for her.

Whatever happens in the scene between them now is free to be whatever they *do* based solely on what they are made to *feel*, created honestly by what they *hear*!

I have developed another exercise that challenges the actor's (bad) habit of preparing how to say a line simply by not giving the actor her lines.

CHAPTER SEVEN

LEARNING TO USE
LISTEN, FEEL, RESPOND

This is an exercise using a script written by Peter DeAnello that helps define and develop the *Listen, Feel, Respond* technique.

As you begin this exercise, *trust* and *acceptance* will be huge issues to tackle.

Imagine receiving a script for which you are to prepare the role of LEE, reading against the role of CONNER. When you are handed the script, you are told you may not prepare with your scene partner and you may not look at your scene partner's script. As you look to the side that you were handed, all of the lines for LEE have been omitted! Surely, the copier or printer was in error.

Your coach informs you there is no print error. You will prepare to deliver your character's responses to the lines of your scene partner's role, working only with what you see printed on the page.

I am not suggesting the use of formal improvisation techniques. I simply removed the assigned character's lines from the page, so that in a two-character scene, the actor receives only the lines of his or her scene partner.

As you look to the next page for the side, read what is on the page and then follow the instructions step by step.

Everything necessary has been provided.
LEE's lines have been removed, but
the spaces for them have not.

The side that I would give to the actor playing the role of LEE will look like this:

INT. OLD WAREHOUSE FREIGHT ELEVATOR

It stops at the sixth floor and the door opens. CONNER exits and walks down a corridor, filled with bookshelves (lined with school text books) towards the black windows. As soon as he turns around the last row of shelves, the butt of a rifle hits Conner in the shoulder and his glasses fly off and to the floor. Conner can no longer see anything but a blur.

                    CONNER
               (Frightened)
          What?! Who is that?!

Conner searches the ground for his broken glasses. A hand ENTERS FRAME and picks them up, knocking the lens out into his hand.

                    LEE (O.S.)
               (Very nervous)

                    CONNER
          Lee? My glasses …

Lee ENTERS FRAME, quickly hiding his rifle.

                    LEE

He helps Conner up.

                    CONNER
          I couldn't find you …Wanted you
          to help me take some pictures from
          this window. Get better shots from
          here than the steps. Guess you
          found it too, huh?

                    LEE

                    CONNER
What time is it?!

                    LEE

Conner hands his camera toward Lee. Lee hesitantly takes it.

                    CONNER
I'll stay with you …

                    LEE
(Explodes looking at his watch)

                    CONNER
(thrown)
But …

                    LEE
(composing himself)

                    CONNER
What's wrong. Lee?

                    LEE

Lee focuses out the window. CROWD SOUNDS BELOW HEIGHTEN

                    CONNER
What's going on?!

                    LEE

                    CONNER
I mean out there …

                    LEE

                    CONNER
Where's my glasses?

                    LEE

Conner is hurt by his friend's words.

                    CONNER
          (Beat—Helpless)
Hardly see without the glasses.

                    LEE
          (Beat)

                    CONNER
          (Dejected)
My dad was right. ...you were just
bein' nice to me. ...that's all.
          (to himself)
I ain't never going to drive...I can't
even see...

He starts down the hall, reaching for the shelves to guide his way. Lee focuses
on Conner, struggling to walk, then at his hands, somewhat still. They suddenly start to shake again. He thinks.

                    LEE

Conner makes his way back. Lee breathes deeply.

                    CONNER
Yeah?

                    LEE

Conner shrugs his shoulders.

>   LEE (cont'd)

>   CONNER
> Till you started here, few weeks back,
> nobody ever really talked to me...

>   LEE
> (Pacing)

>   CONNER
> You weren't just bein' nice, right?
> You really think I can drive?

>   LEE
> (Focused on Conner for the first
>   time—a friend.)

Lee thinks, then checks his hands. They're not shaking anymore)

>   CONNER
> Want I should leave you alone now?

>   LEE
> (Looks out window)

>   CONNER
> Told Sarge all about you.

>   LEE

>   CONNER
> Never learned to say dad...Sarge
> was the first word I ever said...

What everybody else always called
him…In the Army …The Police
force…

                    LEE
        (Looks back, startled)

                    CONNER
Retired.

(END)

Now, the actor who is to prepare LEE seems to have his work cut out for him. Indeed you do. You are the actor preparing for the role of LEE.

Let's go through the learning process of how to use this exercise to your advantage by following the steps carefully. Let go of your expectations.

You will not be able to begin preparation of *how* you will be saying Lee's lines or on what words you will be providing emphasis.

I will begin with the assumption that this technique of preparation is new to you and that having your lines absent from the side is also something that is new to you.

Generally speaking, we all tend to fear what we do not understand and so we have learned to avoid the unknown out of self-preservation. It is natural to try to protect ourselves from something as simple as embarrassment or as complicated as fear of death. In this case, I am hoping it is the former, and nowhere near the latter!

Let's begin exploring this side using the *Listen, Feel, Respond* technique.

The actor must begin by doing what every actor should always do in preparing each script: read the entire side or the entire piece, working to simply understand what you have in your hand.

1. What is the story?
2. What do you know about what you read?

Always begin with *WHAT YOU HEARD*.

What you train yourself to *hear* (or not) has a lot to do with how quickly you will be able to develop this technique. If you enjoy the process of looking at things in unique ways and are able to keep an open mind, you will soon find this technique simple, quick and easy.

Having the stage and character's directions clue you in on how LEE is *feeling* and what he is doing, as well as how he is getting wherever it is that he is going, is of great benefit.

By paying attention to CONNER's lines, you will have a fairly good map of where you are and where you are going.

Look at the first paragraph of the side:

INT. OLD WAREHOUSE FREIGHT ELEVATOR

It stops at the sixth floor and the door opens. CONNER exits and walks down a corridor, filled with bookshelves (lined with school text books) towards the black windows. As soon as he turns around the last row of shelves, the butt of a rifle hits Conner in the shoulder and his glasses fly off and to the floor. Conner can no longer see anything but a blur.

You are given the location/setting and many other clues as to how the scene is to be constructed emotionally, physically and intentionally as well as how the characters will interact, even before they meet.

Let's look deeper.

1. Have you ever been on an old warehouse freight elevator? They are quite different from the comfy, paneled and discreet elevators found in lobbies of hotels and department stores.

2. Freight elevators in old warehouses often have hand-operated gates that must be opened and closed with a large hand strap. They are noisy, large and powerful machines that are designed purely for function, not for aesthetics.

3. If you are paying attention, they smell of hard work, oil, and thick grease and even of electricity that drives them.

4. The wood lined walls are scuffed and marred. The wooden deck has probably been replaced several times and is in a state of disrepair.

5. When the machine begins its task, there is a powerful, electrical force that sends a number of functions into operation simultaneously. The result is the raising or lowering of the car.

6. As the car is raised, the brick walls that separate the elevator shaft from the floors of storage rooms begin to drop away. Slowly at first, but steadily and gently with increasing speed, large openings in the dropping bricks arrive and disappear as the only way to measure which floor you have just passed.

7. As you arrive at the 5th opening, you throttle down the speed of the elevator car, anticipating the opening that will mark the 6th level, on which you will depart.

8. With only one person (LEE) on the 6th floor, it is easy to hear the approaching freight elevator, allowing Lee the time to prepare for the arrival of the elevator.

9. Now, as the behemoth arrives at its destination, the interior protective gates are raised and lowered with a well-rehearsed and confident action. Then the outer doors that keep anyone from falling into the shaft are opened with the same certainty and alarm that informs anyone within a reasonable distance, that the elevator has arrived, carrying with it its operator and any load that might be destined for delivery.

10. Once CONNER has exited the elevator, the outer doors must be closed if anyone else is to use the elevator. Of course if CONNER believes he is the only one working that day, he may opt not to close the doors. At any rate, his arrival is one that is not silent and unnoticed.

11. CONNER then heads to the black windows through a corridor filled with books. The description makes it sound as though it takes a while to get to the last row, doesn't it?

Are you getting the idea? Let's keep going. There are more details that will continue to define relationship, setting, and intention. You are beginning to *listen* with more of your senses to create the immediate and 3-dimensional realism of the setting and relationship as well as the storyline itself.

The two characters have yet to meet in this scene. However, with the attention to the deeper sense of awareness and detail that you are investing in it, you can *hear*, *feel* and *respond* with a much greater understanding of what might happen when and if they do!

12. Can you feel the size of this space? Don't miss the description of *how* he walks. It says, simply, "...CONNER exits and walks down a corridor ..." There is absolutely no indication that he is tentative or uncertain. Therefore, we must assume that Conner is familiar with the space and in turn, conclude that he must work there.

13. Give some thought to the smell of many shelves of books. Can you see what the space must look like if the windows are blackened? It indicates that the sunlight would damage whatever might be stored, so whatever light is provided is either very low or minimal or in some way controlled in order to keep the stored books safe. A storeroom full of books has a certain quality of sound as well. Think about it. Cement floors, tall shelves filled with books. Brick or cement walls decorated with nothing but hallways and content markers.

Now as CONNER innocently and determinedly turns the last corner, he is knocked hard in the shoulder with an object that is known only to the attacker and the viewer, as the butt of a gun. CONNER's glasses, which are as thick as coke bottle bottoms, are jarred free from his face and are thrown to the floor with enough force they are broken beyond repair.

14. What did you *HEAR* when this happened? Did you *hear* the butt of the rifle slamming hard into Conner's shoulder, his "Umph" or grunt as he is hit? Did you hear the sound of his glasses hitting against the cement floor and breaking?

15. The attacker is obviously someone who chooses not to kill the innocent or even injure them. By his method, he has decided only to take advantage of the chance to surprise, and then evaluate the next course of action, depending on whom the intruder might be.

16. With his shoulder in pain, his glasses nowhere to be found, and almost completely blind, CONNER is obviously "Frightened". It is even written in parenthesis in Conner's first line to make sure the actor *gets it.*

Did you *hear* all of that in that first paragraph of description? Sixteen specific and minute details that establish life, relationship, intention, emotion, character, setting, image and even olfactory sensations were contained in that paragraph.

If you missed some, perhaps you were in a hurry to get to the lines. Maybe you wanted to see if what you were to read had any personal interest to you as an actor, like how big was your part, how many lines, etc.

> Developing a deeper sense of *listening* requires that you think in more terms than just what you actually *hear*.

By *listening* to more than just the physical description of setting, you are able to place yourself within the scene. You enable yourself to get inside the scene and live it in real time or even in slow motion, drinking in the opportunities that pass the average reader by.

Now, we hear CONNER ask in a frightened manner, **"What?! Who is that?!"** followed by another descriptive and beneficial note from the author to direct us toward what is most important to see. (Or in *Listen, Feel, Respond*, what we need to *Listen* to.)

Conner searches the ground for his broken glasses. A hand ENTERS FRAME and picks them up, knocking the lens out into his hand.

                    LEE (OS)

Now, it is your turn to write the first line of what you were made to *FEEL*. Write what you *need* to say! (Remember, screenwriting is minimal; characters speak only when and what they need to say, saying only what pictures alone won't tell.)

Go ahead; write the line right into the space provided above, before the end quote. If nothing comes to mind, let's go back and review and then look ahead! What is Conner's response to the line you just wrote (or will write?)

                    CONNER
          Lee? My glasses ...

Lee ENTERS FRAME, quickly hiding his rifle.

OF COURSE! Now, it is beginning to make sense! Conner knows who hit him! He knows it by the sound of Lee's voice.

Lee is seen by the viewer/camera for the first time because he "ENTERS FRAME." We also know that because he hides his rifle, that it is not Conner he is afraid of, nor is Conner the intended enemy, at least for the moment. We may even assume that the two of them are friends. (Of course we find out later that in fact, they are.)

Develop your awareness to recognize facts (or clues) that are provided within the side or material that is given to you. Start with the question, "What do we know?" In other words, look for the facts as they are written.

1. We know that LEE is on the 6th floor of a warehouse for books.
2. We know that Lee is alone and holding a rifle.
3. We know that CONNER is arriving on the same floor wearing glasses that are the only tool that allows him to see clearly where he is going.
4. We know that upon Conner's arrival, he is surprised by a shoulder slam with a rifle butt and that he is now unable to see and is searching for his prized glasses.
5. We know that it is Lee who gives him his glasses, making sure that they are not functional.
6. We know they are not expecting to see each other, but are both on the 6th floor for their own specific and important reasons.

Once you have gone through the script and found as many facts as you think you can, (perhaps there are more than I have listed; or fewer, if you disagree with the ones I have listed) then, it is time to get creative.

Begin the creative process by asking the question, "What can we assume?" We can assume darn near ANYTHING! But if we are going to make sense of this scene and make good enough decisions to have a chance at making the scene work, what assumptions can we make to bridge the gap of what we know and what we have yet to learn?

1. We must assume that Lee and Conner are friends.
2. If there is any doubt, always re-read the entire side to see if that decision checks out.
3. We learn later on in the side, that the fact that they are friends is indeed paramount to the story's development.

If you missed the proof, here it is. It is one of the lines that Conner says to Lee:

CONNER
  Till you started here, few weeks back,
  nobody ever really talked to me...

Now you are beginning to understand how important it is to pay attention not only to *minute* details, but also to consider the *whole* of a piece in order to begin to make solid, effective choices in *who* you are, *what* you want and *how* you will go about achieving your goals.

Re-read just the first descriptive paragraph of the scene between Lee and Conner again, allowing yourself to *Listen* to everything that is between the lines, as described above. You will automatically begin to *FEEL* emotions that were previously non-existent.

Have you written LEE's first line in yet? If not, be sure to go back and do that.

Having read the entire side at least once, even though your (LEE's) lines don't exist, connecting your senses (both physical and intuitive) to the words and descriptive details that are available, you should get a fair sense of most everything you need to construct the scene.

Follow the examples on how to develop the lines for LEE as you progress through the entire side.

But let's not forget his scene partner who will be playing CONNER. Let's take a look at his side:

Note to the reader: You may want to avoid reading ahead at this point until you have constructed LEE's lines as you are made to *feel*. Your *reactions* to what you are made to *feel* created by what you *heard* (or *Listened* to) are the lines of LEE's dialogue that you should trust and write down, before you go on to read what LEE's actual lines are.

Of course, it is best to give the next section to a scene partner to do with LEE's lines, the same thing you just did with CONNER. Assuming that is what you will do, once you have both filled in the lines for the character you are developing, see if you can run the scene with what you two have written.

There will be sections that may not play well, but usually, if the scene directions and clues have been carefully diagnosed as directed in the points given above, you will discover that the words you wrote will fit quite nicely.

Finally, exchange scripts and perform your lines as the author wrote them. You will smile almost uncontrollably at the clarity and familiarity you have with the piece. Because you don't have your partner's lines, you will be allowed to *listen* more effectively and efficiently than before.

Note to the reader: The actor preparing for CONNER will take this side to prepare, while you are preparing LEE.

INT. OLD WAREHOUSE FREIGHT ELEVATOR

It stops at the sixth floor and the door opens. CONNER exits and walks down a corridor, filled with bookshelves (lined with school text books) towards the black windows. As soon as he turns around the last row of shelves, the butt of a rifle hits Conner in the shoulder and his glasses fly off and to the floor. Conner can no longer see anything but a blur.

> CONNER
> (Frightened)

Conner searches the ground for his broken glasses. A hand ENTERS FRAME and picks them up, knocking the lens out into his hand.

> LEE (O.S.)
> (Very nervous)
> God, I'm sorry, Conner...you scared me...snuck
> up on me.

> CONNER

Lee ENTERS FRAME, quickly hiding his rifle.

> LEE
> Gee, Conner, they broke...I'm really sorry ...
> What are you doing here, anyway? ...I thought
> you were watching the motorcade from the steps.

He helps Conner up.

> CONNER

                    LEE
Uh …Yeah ….

                    CONNER

                    LEE
Twelve twenty-five. …Look, why don't you
leave the camera with me and go on down to the
steps …It's closer …I'll get the shots for
you, okay?

Conner hands his camera toward Lee. Lee hesitantly takes it.

                    CONNER

                    LEE
          (Explodes looking at his watch)
You can't!

                    CONNER
          (thrown)

                    LEE
          (Composing himself)
Conner, you can't be here…I need time to
myself…

                    CONNER

                    LEE
Nothing…just had a fight with Marina …
We're having some problems and I need to
be alone to think.

Lee focuses out the window. CROWD SOUNDS BELOW HEIGHTEN

                    CONNER

                    LEE

I ...may not be going back home for a
while is all ...

                    CONNER

                    LEE
Oh ...Nothin' ...yet.

                    CONNER

                    LEE
Broken, I said! Now, get out of here!

Conner is hurt by his friends' words.

                    CONNER
                 (Beat. Helpless)

                    LEE
                 (Beat)
Look ...I'll buy you a new pair of
glasses tomorrow, alright?

                    CONNER
                 (dejected)

He starts down the hall, reaching for the shelves to guide his way. Lee focuses
on Conner, struggling to walk, then at his hands, somewhat still. They suddenly start to shake again. He thinks.

               LEE
Conner …C'mere for a minute.

               CONNER

Conner makes his way back. Lee breathes deeply.

               CONNER

               LEE
We're pals, right?

Conner shrugs his shoulders.

               LEE (cont'd)
You're the only guy here with some real
substance. Honest.

               CONNER

               LEE
               (pacing)
World's filled with ignorance.

               CONNER

               LEE
               (Focused on Conner for the first time—a friend)
I meant that. You're not so different than
Everybody else. Conner …you just let
people tell you that …Lots of people out
there driving that shouldn't even have
licenses …I think it'll be a good thing for
you …

Lee thinks, then checks his hands. They're not shaking anymore.

                    CONNER

                    LEE
               (looks out the window)
          Not yet …Couple a more minutes.

                    CONNER

                    LEE
          Why do you call your dad Sarge?

                    CONNER

                    LEE
               (looks back, startled)
          Your dad's a cop?

                    CONNER

(END)

Fill in the blanks with what you are made to *feel*. Go back and re-read this chapter to remind you of the process.

In most cases, the feeling-driven lines the actors invent, are very similar to what the author wrote. The intention of the lines is understood through relationship; NOT based solely on what each actor has to say.

**Actors who prepare how they are going to say their lines
cut off any sense of truth and
limit their ability to take direction.**

If you choose to have the actors read the scene as they wrote their lines, great. Then, be sure to have the two actors switch their scripts ...now having only their lines on the page. This will keep them from reading their scene partners' lines, greatly improving their cold-read technique, as well as strengthening their ability to listen.

If you want another opportunity to explore using the technique of *Listen, Feel, Respond* to fill in the blanks, here's one that gives you nothing except two characters.

There are no stage or character descriptions or directions …YOU fill in the blanks based on what you *hear* and how you are made to *feel*.

1: Hey.

2:

1: What's up?

2:

1: Did you sleep alright?

2:

1: Well, what do you think we should do?

2:

1: Come on, stop it! Just talk to me.

2:

1: Oh no, it's up to you.

2:

1: You would.

2:

1: Bullshit.

2:

1: Tell me about it. Look, whether you understand it or not, I do. God, I can't believe we're fighting about this. You know how I feel, don't you?

2:

1: Me too.

2:

1: Right now?

2:

1: I love you.

2:

END.

I am not going to provide you with the second character's lines because I would love to see how many ways you are willing to change the course of the storyline without the author defining that for you.

Tell you what. If you will send me what you filled in, I will send you what the author wrote.

As you work on this exercise you are developing several skills that will serve you well as an actor:

1. Concentration.
2. Confidence.
3. Decision Making.
4. Creativity.
5. Commitment.

Moreover, you are developing trust in all of the skills listed above. As an actor, your ideas, decisions and skills are valuable and effective when they are finely tuned to the whole and entire project.

Suggestions that actors make when they do not know the entire story are often little more than trouble. The suggestions may serve the individual, but without regard to the story, the relationship and/or to the overall intent, the suggestions are at best selfish and ignorant.

Having accomplished these exercises designed to exemplify the *response* of *Listen, Feel, Respond*, let's use the tools you have now to work with a side that you might get for an audition.

CHAPTER EIGHT

PREPARING AUDITION SIDES

Peter DeAnello wrote a number of screenplays that I am hoping we can one day produce. In the meantime, they serve this subject well and I am grateful for his allowing me their use.

Generally, when sides are made available to the actor, the entire screenplay is not available and so it is important to be able to make solid, believable decisions with very little information. Enough information is available when you know how to see it and know *how* to use it.

You will read the next side three times through in the following manner:

1.) Read through the side the first time for the story.

2.) Read through it the second time to study the relationship between Charles and Elizabeth.

3.) Read through it the third time to *Listen* to what the character opposite to the character you have chosen, wants from you.

This side comes from a piece entitled *SEASONS*.

CHARLES and ELIZABETH are playing the outfield on a corporate softball team. Running, to catch a high, fly ball, they have run into and knocked each other down. Elizabeth's knee is injured and they have been arguing about who was in whose way.

CHARLES
Tell me something. Is it all men you hate, or just ...

ELIZABETH
You.

CHARLES
I feel better for the men of the world.

ELIZABETH
Damn corporate yuppie.

CHARLES
Excuse me?

ELIZABETH
You heard me. You're all the same.

CHARLES
Does that mean all men, or all yuppies?

ELIZABETH
All those who fall under the heading, "Corporate Yuppie".

CHARLES
Oh ...I just wanted to clear that up. Continue please.

ELIZABETH
You think you're so cocky...you're all the same...
comfortable in your corporate looking clothes, driving
your corporate cars, climbing your kiss-ass corporate
ladder ...And meanwhile, you forget all about your
corporate families.

CHARLES
Thank you for your corporate views. ...and what do
you do for a living?

ELIZABETH
I teach.

CHARLES
My condolences to the youth of America. What do
you teach? Kamikaze 101?

ELIZABETH
Philosophy in Business Management. "The
Importance of Striving For Independence In A
Corporate Society."

CHARLES
Look, you don't know me. So why don't you keep
your judgments to yourself? I don't even know why
I'm still here! First, you run into me, then you blame
me for it, and then you abuse me! What are you
doing here anyway? Who invited you?

ELIZABETH
My father knows I love to play softball.

CHARLES
Who is he? Does he work for Lanfield and Lanfield?
Because if he does, I'd like to give him a good piece
of my mind! I'd like to ruin his Sunday! I'd like
him to know...

ELIZABETH
Why don't you do that? Let him have it with both
barrels! Tell him how his nasty daughter got in the
way of your moment of glory and just ruined your
whole day! And, before he fires you, you also have
my permission, and make sure you don't misquote
me, to tell him everything I said about "Corporate
Yuppies!" And while you're on a roll, I'd appreciate
if you'd further brighten his day with the thought that
his daughter thinks she's an idiot for visiting in the
first place because he never had time for her when she
lived here ...I should have known, nothing would
change ...I'll be behind you all the way, I promise.

CHARLES
Fire me, huh? What does your father do for Lanfield
and Lanfield?

ELIZABETH
My father is Lanfield and Lanfield… The first one,
anyway. The second is my uncle.

CHARLES
Oh …
(trying to save face)
You think you've got me pegged, don't you? So what
if your father signs my checks! So what if I'd lose my
new Beemer, my condo on the beach, and my eight
week old Golden retriever, Fred! It would all be worth
it, because I am a man of principle! You're wrong! So,
if you want to go crying to daddy, go right ahead,
because there are other jobs, and I won't miss all those
things one bit!
(pause)
Honestly, I would miss Fred. …he's so cute and
loyal…he has these little crossed eyes …Got him
cheaper, because of that. He's fine, just looks a little
funny.

ELIZABETH
…Sounds like Fred is a good friend.

CHARLES
Yeah.

ELIZABETH
I promise to make sure he gets a good home.

CHARLES
Thanks.
(starts to leave and stops)
I can't.

ELIZABETH
Forget something?

CHARLES
Look, I may be dirt in your eyes and in your

fathers, but I know what kind of person I am and
that's all that counts.

                    ELIZABETH
So?

                    CHARLES
So, let me at least help you to your car.

                    ELIZABETH
I'll go to the emergency room.

                    CHARLES
Good.

                    ELIZABETH
Only if you come with me.

END.

Having read this scene now, for the first time, ask yourself the following
questions:

1. What have you discovered about the storyline?
2. Storylines have a lot to do with how you will play your role. What is the
    genre? (comedy, drama, sitcom, etc.)
3. What is your first impression? Summarize the storyline in one sentence.
4. Now go back and read the side again. This time, *listen* to the relationship.
5. How does the relationship affect the storyline?

You may find that by making a *sarcastic* choice instead of an *angry* choice
you will tell the same story in a different way.

6. Compare an *insecure* choice against a *confident* choice. Wherever there is
    love, indifference, pain, joy, or any of the many other choices I gave you
    to use in the list of emotions, use the emotional list to specifically define
    your choice of intention.

7. Finally, if you are preparing to perform the role of Charles, start reading the side again, for the third time, paying particular attention to Elizabeth's point of view.

8. How does Elizabeth respond to you? (Charles).

9. What does Elizabeth want from you?

After completing these given steps, you are now ready to cold read for Charles.

You have spent the majority of your time getting to know your scene partner's role, but what you will discover is that when you read the scene, your lines will be fresh, new and more present.

Words and reactions may even surprise you, as the scripted words may not match what you would say to Elizabeth. When we converse naturally, we often say less than what we feel, but we may also say more than we meant to. Either way, it creates obstacles and challenges that must be dealt with immediately and in the moment.

Compare the actor who prepares in this way to the actor who spends the same five minutes of preparation looking only at his lines and how he plans on saying them. The comparison is like day to night.

Waiting for your cue to say your line and then saying it with a rehearsed and prepared inflection, intention and force, inhibits any opportunity to make discoveries or to react spontaneously to the moment at hand.

CHAPTER NINE

SUMMARY OF
LISTEN, FEEL, RESPOND

One of the most valuable and important skills in acting is the ability to take direction. It is the single most important reason than I can think of for any actor to continue her search and application of new studies.

Being prepared with creative and fitting ideas for a rehearsal, cold read, audition or performance, reflects preparedness, accountability and professionalism to any auditor, director or individual interested in hiring you as talent.

I hope that you will read the chapters on *Listen, Feel, Respond* many times over. Like any new theory or lesson, it takes several times to absorb, several more to understand and then a few more to apply and perfect.

Having worked with hundreds of students over the past twenty years, I am proud to have met and worked with each one. If you are one of those students, I hope that you are still using the skills you invested in. This review will bring back lots of memories of my asking, "What did you hear?"

What you listen to has a profound effect on what you hear. How you listen defines and produces an immediate effect on what you feel.

CHAPTER TEN

REQUIRED TOOLS OF THE PROFESSIONAL ACTOR

THE MOST IMPORTANT TOOLS: YOUR MIND & BODY

Now let's talk about a tool that is not, perhaps, so obvious, but is certainly one you could not do this craft without: You! Specifically, I'm referring to your mind and your body.

If you hire a carpenter to build an addition onto your home, would you expect the laborers to come with their tools in hand? Would you expect that the carpenter and his laborers would know how to use their tools?

And what about those tools? A carpenter, no matter how good, would have a very difficult time cutting a board if the blade on his saw was dull or broken. He would not be able to drive a Phillips head screw with a blade head screwdriver.

It is no different for the person who chooses to advertise himself or herself as a professional actor.

Typically, people who call themselves actors have spent some time on the stage, have done a few plays or have had some success at public speaking and have gotten the bug to do more. Eventually, friends and family encourage them to continue with their acting and speaking skills.

This is where the serious either rise up or give up.

Whereas the serious will seek out whatever means necessary to develop their natural-born desire and skills, the majority, will be content to do as little as possible, expecting their skills and abilities to develop through some magical means of osmosis or observation alone.

We have all heard the phrase, *Use it or lose it*. Nothing could be more useful to the actor than to apply the knowledge of that simple statement. Either you choose to stay fit through proper diet and exercise, or you choose not to. Either you choose to continue to feed your brain stimulus, making it work efficiently and properly, or you choose not to.

Many weekend carpenters have been known to build an addition, just as weekend actors who have some other profession are in their community play-house productions. The question is:

> ## Are you a clerk who does some acting, or are you an actor who is able to multi-task?

Actors who multi-task will do whatever they must to put food on their table and a roof over their heads until they can, eventually, let go of whatever means they had as support and go solo with acting or a combination of acting, producing, editing, writing, etc.

When I was working at other jobs to support my habit (of acting), I never took my mind off of what I really wanted. I wanted simply to act. Day and night, I thought about what it must be like to be able to get up and study a script, or go to the gym or to go to the theatre or to a set.

I took only the jobs that would allow me to go to auditions and would allow me time to be gone for jobs. There was never enough money for vacations, dates, movies or anything, except to pay whatever meager debts I owed to the shared rent & utilities. Yet when people asked what I did, I never replied, "I scrub exhaust vents." I would say, "I am an actor."

When you make a public statement that you are an actor, you are choosing to create in your mind as well as in the minds of all others whom you tell, that you are either going to keep your word or you are not.

You have already committed to being an actor simply by voicing it. Now, it is time to keep your word. Pick up a biography or an autobiography of actors or industry-related persons that you admire, even if you know nothing about them. Check in with the production companies listed in your phone book or in your area's film and stage-production guides and ask what tasks you might be able to fill as an intern. If no intern positions are available, ask whether or not you can sweep the floors. Do whatever is necessary to keep your word: that you are indeed a working actor.

When you are focused on a goal or a decision, you will find that everything you are doing to achieve that goal will become so much easier and enjoyable.

I have very fond memories of having worked at a Dairy Queen for several years while striving to free myself to become a full-time actor. My bosses, Rick and Denise Slater, were my best friends to whom I will be forever grateful. They gave me tremendous latitude in my scheduling because they understood my passion and determination for my dream. They had the same zeal and devotion to their dream and we often sat up nights together, eagerly sharing our personal goals. We would laugh and cajole each other about what we were doing to achieve those goals.

Take a moment and think about your situation. Do you have a job that enables you to develop your true career? Perhaps you find yourself in a job like the one I had scrubbing exhaust vents. My boss at that company had no idea what my goals were and didn't care. It was all about *his* business. I was there to live and perform his dream, not mine. The work was hot and dangerous as we sprayed caustic soda up into hot, dirty and oil-laden restaurant exhaust vents after the kitchen had closed for the night. The late hours and the higher pay made it possible for me to be in theater, but neither of those *assets* served my dream as well as the flexible schedule and supportive employers at Dairy Queen. If this sounds familiar, get moving *now* to break out of your stultifying situation.

> When you are able to spend less time making excuses for doing
> what you *must,* and more time doing what you *love,*
> then you will know you are on the right track.
> What are you doing to work towards your goal?

Now that you have chosen to make acting your profession, let's talk about the more tangible tools that are required for the professional.

CHAPTER ELEVEN

HEADSHOTS

What makes a good headshot, demo reel or any other tool that will be used in promoting you? Definitely **not** that photograph you had taken for your senior class annual.

I know, I know you spent an entire day at the salon to get your hair, face, & nails just right! And that is precisely my point. Is that what you will do before going out *every* day? Before *every* audition? Is that how you make yourself look each and every day you appear in public? If you answered yes to all of these questions above, then perhaps that *Glamour* shot you had taken will work just fine.

For the rest of you (like me) you will want a professionally prepared and carefully planned session with a photographer that your agent (or prospective agents) will recommend. "Wait a minute," you say. "That photo has been used for every performance since foot lights went electric."

Let's start by discussing the purpose of a headshot. It is your most important calling card. It is your first impression to that person you want to have shake your hand and welcome you to her production.

If you are just getting started in this business, you may still be unaware of just how business-like this business is. So let's look at this from a casting director's point of view.

ABC Company has hired X producer to create a commercial to sell their widget. The producer then calls a casting company to suggest the perfect actor for the Widget spot.

ABC Company wants a specific individual that will appeal to the specific market that will buy their Widget. For the sake of example only, let's say the widget is a female's personal product. We know now that men will not be asked to this audition and that children and older women are also exempt.

So the casting company is going to contact the actors' agencies they regularly work with to suggest they send pictures of the appropriate *age* and *type* actors for the upcoming audition.

This is where you will succeed or fail before you may ever know it. Your agent has been bugging you to update your headshot for over a year. Your hair is longer, your teeth are straighter, your eyes sparkle more with experience, and you have lost 25 pounds.

> The picture you couldn't afford to update has just cost you far more than a photographer's fee.

You may be perfect for the role, but if your picture does not reflect that, it's no good.

Another scenario:

Let's say you heard about the casting through the grapevine. You have let yourself go, you have gained 25 pounds, your hair is starting to gray, and smoking has aged your skin into a wrinkled leathery mess. You submit your 5-year-old photo and the casting company says, "Yes! She's perfect! Where has she been? The ABC Company will love her!" You are called in to read—and the shock that you see on the Casting Director's face is not the reaction you were expecting. And I can assure you, the look of your face is not what they had in mind either!

If you are LUCKY, the ABC Company will not be at the read. (I'll explain later.)

More often than not, the Casting Company will have you read on camera and will say a kind "Thank you" as they usher you out the door. Your audition was never recorded and your photo will go in the trash, or mounted on the DON'T EVER CALL AGAIN file. Your mistake will spread through every Producer's cocktail party from here to there and back again.

Certainly not the way you want to be spoken of, or the way you want to be remembered!

It's a very good idea to consult with professionals in the film and television industry as to what they look for in photos. Ask to look at their talent files and look for individuals in your age and type categories who work often. Note the lighting, the background, the body language, the expression, everything you can about the photos and discuss these topics with your agent, the photographer, and if possible, casting agents and producers.

So you can see this process of just getting your headshot taken is one that deserves a great deal of thought, preparation, and discernment. Once you have done your homework, the session will go much easier and with greater results and satisfaction than what you would otherwise have known or believed.

Earlier, I had mentioned that if you were lucky, the client (ABC Company) would not be in for your casting call. You may wonder why that would be beneficial.

> Your first impression is lasting and important.
> You must look like your photograph.
> The person in your photo is who the casting director is expecting to meet.

If you have gained or lost a lot of weight, changed your hair, or have aged since your photo was taken, and you no longer look like your photo, not only have you wasted their time, you have proven yourself an amateur.

Black and White (B&W) or Color? 8" X 10" or 8 1/2" X 11"?

The standard by which the industry has always operated is 8 X 10 B&W. Your agent and other industry persons may well say… "Sure, color on 8 1/2 X 11 is fine." But I repeat…. The industry standard has always been 8 X 10 B&W.

With the increasing accessibility to the Internet, this is your perfect chance to put up your own web site and list the address on your resume. With a simple click anyone can access as many photos both color & B&W as your web site will allow. More and more jobs are being earned from a casting director or client seeing you on the web!

Let's talk first about what goes on the reverse of your headshot, an equally important tool: your resume.

CHAPTER TWELVE

RESUME

A resume, first and foremost, should always be truthful, reflecting only what you have actually done and what you are certified to do.

At the very least, if you present false credits it will establish you firmly amongst the burgeoning crowd of boastful, insecure, fear-filled wanna-be's who call themselves actors.

At worst, it could land you in the hospital or even cost you your life, to say nothing of the problems it will create for the company that hires you expecting you to be able to do what you have claimed.

"Wait a minute," you say. "Cost me my life?!"

If you list on your resume that you can scuba dive, simply because you love the water and believe that you would be able to do it if necessary, such a boastful, ignorant mistake could indeed be extremely dangerous.

Many students come to me with claims they have nothing to put on their resume. Wearing a look of defeat, anxiety and depression they slowly sink to the ground, having voiced their empty insecurities.

My response is always: Hogwash! You have a name. That goes at the top. If you are a member of any union(s) put that next. You have a weight, hair color, eye color and height. Those are listed next. Unless your agent specifically asks you to put your age on your resume, you are better off omitting that entirely.

Next comes the listing of everything you have ever done. Assuming you are just getting started, this may be possible to do. Don't be afraid to include that school play, the speech you gave to the Rotary Club, and the bit part in the industrial training video. However, if you have been doing this a while, you know that you can't fit everything you have ever done onto the back of an 8x10 photo. It won't take long before you can be selective with your resume.

Your resume should look different from the resume of a stage actor. You will need to divide your experience into categories. Let's take a look at the categories of a film/video actor's resume in the order that they should appear.

FILM

Remember, this resume is for the camera, not for the stage, so you want to list the FILMS you have appeared in first. If you haven't been in any films, don't panic. Just leave this heading and section off your resume until you are in one. FILM is still considered celluloid; you know, the super 8mm, 8mm, super 16mm, 16mm and 35mm stock that runs through the camera at 24 frames per second (fps), as opposed to the much less expensive video.*

I am tempted to explain the differences here between film & video because such things intrigue me. However, if you are also interested, you are probably already aware of the many differences and of the new technologies, so I will leave that for another book and another time.

If your local University or Educational facility hosts a film-making program, and the students are being taught film production and have access to you as an actor, this is your best introduction to being in films. DO IT. Then, you can add a FILM credit to your resume.

Like all listings to follow, the *formula* for listing your credits is as follows:

1. List the film (or commercial or industrial or program) title Left Justified.

2. List the character name, title or description Center Justified.

3. List the Production Company and Director's name Right Justified.

TELEVISION

Following the FILM heading, you will want to list all of your television appearances under TELEVISION. What? You haven't appeared in one of those *reality* programs? You haven't been seen on TV wearing a chicken outfit selling nuggets? Don't despair. Again, just skip this heading and move on to the next.

INDUSTRIAL

Following the heading, TELEVISION, this category is where you will most likely start your resume if you are just getting a start. Under Industrial, you can list anything and everything that you have ever appeared in on camera. No, I'm not suggesting those family videos, but anything that has ever been done by a student or a professional with intent to screen, distribute or publicly display the end result.

The INDUSTRIAL heading is best used for those corporate training films where you appear as the spokesperson. You may have appeared as *background* or as an *extra* in one of these videos that are used at trade shows or are introducing new services or products of a corporation in their in-house videos. In short, industrial projects are produced to serve as educational, informational or even as entertainment for a one-time screening or as in-house, on-going training tool for a specific group or organization.

THEATRE

You still haven't done any of the above roles? Well, put the knife back in the drawer and roll your sleeves back down, there is still something you can do to have a resume. It is the heading entitled: THEATRE. This, of course, is the heading that includes any and all listings of anything and everything you have ever performed publicly, anywhere, with anyone. A role as simple as the Tree in the interpretive dance show you did in the production, *Save Our Forests* for Greentrees will do. Call up every performance in grade school, include what you are doing with your community theatre group, or use your imagination. But be honest.

Still nothing? Okay, now get the knife. I'm kidding! Following all of these categories, it is time to list what skills you may have that can be used to the benefit of any one of a million special interests. The heading is simply: SPECIAL SKILLS.

SPECIAL SKILLS

Are you a certified diver? Can you jump horses? Are you a body builder? Skate boarder? BMX'r? How many languages do you read and speak fluently? How many dialects? Do you juggle? Perform Martial Arts? Dance? Sky dive? Rock climb? Ice skate? Water ski? Downhill ski? Box? Are you a gymnast? Do you bend it like Beckham? One of the most successful and valuable skills of one of my former students was that he was a professional mascot for a major league baseball team. That single listing got him in more doors than you can swing a stick at.

EDUCATION

If you still need a heading to help fill out a barren resume, you can list one more heading entitled: EDUCATION or TRAINING. Herein you would list the schools and programs where you learned any and all of the skills you mentioned above.

It should be noted that the resume shown is a basic outline for you to follow when typing up your resume.

You can design your own layout as long as it flows in the given basic formula, and is neat and easy to read. Depending on how savvy you are in using your computer (or how much money you want to save), here are a few good ideas:

1. Create and save your Resume in a word-processing file that allows for easy updates.

2. Print the resume directly onto the back of your 8x10 photo.

3. In many markets, it is acceptable to import small character shots along side your resume to give auditors an idea of your different looks.

4. If you do not print directly to the back of your headshot, be sure to trim and attach each resume to each photo. NEVER give your agent separate photos from your resumes, or ones that are not trimmed and neat!

On the next page is one example of how a working film actor's resume can look. The agent that signs you may have a format that they would prefer, so be sure to ask before making too many copies.

YOUR NAME

SAG/AFTRA

Agency Name

Agent's Name

(123) 456-7891

Height: 5'11"

Weight: 180

Hair: Brown

Eyes: Blue

FILM

Title	Character Name	Production Co. Name/Name of Director
Wunmore Movie	Deputy	Starwest Productions/S. Pettit, Director
Wonton Women	Lonely Man	Winsatyre Prod./B. Dover, Director
Workinatit	Jerry	CFI Studio/Chad Schnackel, Director
Stopit	extra	Your University/Ferd Berfull, Director

COMMERCIAL/TELEVISION

Yellow River	Faucet, the Engineer	Runon Prod./I.P. Daly, Dir.
I M 4 U	N.M.E.	Anacronym Studios/R. U. Kidding, Dir.
Show Off	Principle Dancer	Havin'a Ball Productions/Rollin Uphill, Dir.

INDUSTRIAL

Jumping Cliffs	Jack B. Nimble	Riss Key Images/Hugo First, Director
Secrets to Success	Spokesman	Action Plan Studios/Ken U. Keepah, Dir.
Beds R Us	Background	Cloud 9 Productions/Lee Dng Sheyp, Dir.

THEATRE

Twelfth Night	Malvolio	Upstart Players/Richard Smith, Director
Godspell	John/Judas	Longstudy Playhouse/Joan Laurence, Dir.
Dirty Work at the Crossroad	Villain	Summ Playhouse/Merna Pritchard, Dir.
Glass Menagerie	Tom	Yourown College/Dr. Know Itall
Fiddler on the Roof	Constable	Yourown College/Dr. Know Itall
Grease	Chorus	Mione High School/Hugh R. Bitten
Man of La Mancha	Sancho	Mione High School/Hugh R. Bitten

SPECIAL SKILLS

Certified Scuba Instructor   Jazz Trumpet   Percussion/Drums   Skateboard Awards
Tenor   Sword Swallower   Juggler   Fire Breather   Balloon Clown
Whistler   Gymnast   Read and Speak Fluent: German, French and Spanish
Dialects: Southern - Mississippi, Georgia, Carolina's.   Texan   North/East-Maine

TRAINING

Superstar Studios	On-Camera & Cold Read Techniques	Anytown, USA—Instructor
Act Out Studio	Commercial On Camera	Anytown, USA—Coach
BePro Workshop	Interview Technique Production Skills	Anytown, USA—Instructor

If you are still uncertain about what to put in your resume, I might suggest you go back and re-read the information provided until you unlock your left-brain sarcophagus and find yourself sorting through the mountain of information you've assembled for your resume.

You can also use your search engine (my favorite is www.dogpile.com) and type in *acting resume*. Your search will render a number of pay-for-information sites, but among them are a number of FREE sites, with great and informative pages.

CHAPTER THIRTEEN

DEMO REEL

Having a demo reel (a video or digital *reel* that lasts less than 3 minutes, demonstrating your skills) can mean the difference between getting the job and losing the job. It is a tool that can get you in doors you would not otherwise know exist. A demo reel, next to your resume and headshot, is one of the most effective ways of showing (literally) what you are capable of.

For every job that you secure, you need to be very aggressive in collecting the work that you do on camera. Collecting the copies is NOT the job of your agent or of anyone but YOU!

Take a notebook, your palm pilot or whatever means you have to record important information and ask who the editor on the project will be. If it is a student or low-budget production, the editor may be the same person who is directing, producing and doing everything.

In any case, if the person who will be editing is available on set, wait until that person is on break, or is not focused on his job, then ask him for his business card or the best way to contact him to obtain a copy of your work.

One of the easiest ways of collecting the work nowadays, is to ask for a DVD, It is easy to carry a blank mini DV tape with you in a self-addressed, postage-paid envelope to hand them as well.
Always have the media you hand them clearly marked with your name, address, and phone number. You are not the only actor/talent that will be asking them for this valuable information.

It is always a good idea to find out what vice the editor may have, and gift them for their extended effort. Chocolates, wine, round trip airfare to Paris, etc. But seriously, a little extra kindness always goes a long way, especially since you will more than likely work with them again, and next time they may not even charge you the dubbing fee.

As you build a good collection of your work, you will want to take a good look at your material with several friends that you have made in the industry, to sort out the scenes and the images. Sometimes just a simple look speaks a thousand words. Discuss which ones show your greatest range and ability.

Next, contact a good editor. Ask around. Get names of those who are trusted, capable and great with what they do. This is not a job for your first attempt with that new editing software you just purchased.

Your reel should not be over 3 minutes in length. Start the reel with your name made very prominent, perhaps with a clear image of your face so that a memorable connection is made with the viewer as to who it is they are watching. Keep the clips short, and keep it moving. Like any powerful and memorable commercial, your goal is to leave the viewer wanting more!

Dramatic scenes often run way too long and the viewer will leave the reel to do something else. Usually these are very busy people who will be watching your reel and they multi-task constantly. Do not expect they will watch your reel like your best friend or lover would.

The last fifteen seconds or so should be a clear and memorable closing that depicts your agent's contact information. (Name and phone number)

If you have a web site, ask the editor doing your reel if they can stream your demo on your web site. In addition, have lots of CD's both pocket size and standard size available to clip to your headshot resume when you arrive at auditions. VHS copies are still acceptable as well. Always have the jackets and media clearly marked with your name and your agent's contact numbers.

CHAPTER FOURTEEN

MOBILE PHONE

My partner, Peter DeAnello who operates Big Fish Talent Agency, tells a great story about the value of a mobile phone.

Peter will stand before a group of actors at any Sunday night showcase, hold up his mobile phone and ask, "How much would you pay for one of these?" Answers range from whatever the most recent provider is selling them for, or even free when you purchase the calling plan, up to maybe one hundred dollars.

Once all of the answers have been given, Peter explains that one of the actors just paid the remarkable fee of five thousand dollars. Following a dramatic pause filled with disbelief from the group, he goes on to say, "That is what an actor lost, when a producer who needed this performer immediately was unable to reach that talent for more than a day and a half."

Twenty years ago, pagers were the rave. Cell phones were outrageously priced huge, heavy pieces of equipment. (They still are referred to as *bricks*.) But today, as communications and technology continue to improve at an immeasurable rate, it is more and more important to be available NOW. When I am preparing to go in to a mid-day movie, I will call my agent just to let him know I'll be busy for those couple of hours, then set the ring to vibrate.

Let me share with you how that actor who was unreachable lost much more than the money. This actor basically destroyed the confidence he had with the producer. You better know that that producer had to work much longer that day to secure talent for the shoot and probably has told the story of whom he lost and what it cost him, to many others in the industry. Now that actor's name is recognized as "un-reliable"!

Equally important for you to know is that the actor's agent lost his percentage of the income; money that agent depends upon to pay his bills ...office, telephones, heating, electric, etc., not to mention, feed his family. That actor just took money out of his agent's pocket.

No legitimate agent ever makes a dime until you make a dollar. If you prove difficult, ask yourself why should an agent work for you?

Have a professional greeting on your answering message. Unless you make your living as a singer, do not make the caller sit through your latest rendition of *You've Got A Friend.*
Do not make the caller wait for a punch line to some inside joke, or anything but your professional greeting.
Simple is best.

CHAPTER FIFTEEN

THE AUDITION

What is your mindset when you are reading for the part? Are you prepared? Are you open? Are you listening?

> If you have been selected from among the hundreds or thousands to read for the part, you have the job.

Look at it this way: If you were the casting director how much time would you like to spend looking at and dealing with incompetent, ignorant, time-wasting, ill-mannered dead beats? (Okay, okay ...you are not that bad. Don't give up your dream yet. I just thought I would wake you up ...you have been reading quite a bit so far.) But believe it or not, the future and success of a casting director is as volatile as yours. They are only as good as the last project they cast. Let's all do everything we can to make each other look good and the marketplace will *dramatically* improve.

In all my years, I have never heard a legitimate casting director and/or a client say, "Hey, let's see how many bad actors we can find in this city. It might be worth a few laughs."

Having selected you from the mountains of headshots and recommendations, the casting director is anxious to have you prove your worth to show their client.

Are you ready? Let's make sure you are. You have your perfect headshot with your honest and clear resume attached on the reverse and you show up ten minutes before your call time to settle in and prepare.

As soon as you open the door to the office where you were called to read, you see the sign-in sheet and 30 other people who look exactly, if not very similar, to you, and they are all eye-balling you.

> Those who are ready will rise quickly to the top;
> those who are not will pray for a miracle.

As a side note, prayer and meditation are never dismissed as bad things and are useful in any situation.

That said, you might be given a sheet that asks for all of your vitals. Vitals are your name, agency, social security number, all of your phone numbers, height, weight, clothing sizes and sometimes, age.

What you write down on that sheet explains who you are represented by (agent) and how best to contact you.

If your agent sent you, DO NOT put your home address or home phone number on any cold call sheet EVER. (Even if it asks for it.) And especially, never put down your Social Security number.

Do submit the agency's name, address and phone number(s) under your name. That way you will avoid all sorts of potential problems.

The best way to avoid being taken advantage of is to always defer to your agent. If the casting call proves to be successful and the casting company does want to have you return either for a callback or to contact you for the job, then your agent will provide them the missing information, or will contact you to approve your giving them whatever information they will need.

If you are represented by an agent, be sure to submit only your agent's contact information when you choose to answer casting calls from posted bills, advertisements and posters. Then, be sure to let your agent know what you have done and, if possible, who may be calling them about the project.

If you do not have an agent and you are venturing out as an independent, it is best to give out only a business number. Whenever possible avoid giving out your home number and/or personal information. It is too easy to give away too much information and too much money when you do your own negotiating. Be careful.

Okay let's talk about finding agency representation and procuring the best agent for you.

CHAPTER SIXTEEN

SECURING AN AGENT

You must know first, that until you actually do some legitimate and recognized work to prove yourself, you are seen as just another pound puppy. (Cute eyes, but no breeding.)

Rule number one: No legitimate agent or agency will ever ask you for money to sign with him or her.

This is where too many actors, even after reading this, will fall prey to the greedy and slick dream pushers who have picked you out of a thousand people, suggesting you can have what it takes if you will only "sign this contract, take these classes and pay these fees."

Of course in the fine print it will say there are NO GUARANTEES. But you sign the contract anyway, because you have saved your paper route money and everything you have earned from working at the local fast food joint. Perhaps your parents, who always want the best for you but know nothing of this industry, plunk down the three thousand dollars. In six months time you will have lousy headshots, a useless resume and are given second and third hand advice from an acting coach who has little more experience than you.

You find that every audition you are sent on, (if you are sent at all) is an open casting call for a job that offers little or no pay, and was listed in the same rag you were reading when you first read your new agent's advertisement on how they would make you a star.

Now, you fear any relationship at all with any coach or agent and become determined to do it all on your own from now on, and the cycle of mistrust and self-preservation over the chance to do the work leads to greater and greater misfortune and/or failure.

Let's stop and get real about this *getting an agent* thing right now.

Every town and every market in the world is *always* looking for *new* and *fresh* faces. If you are coming from a background and history of legitimate stage and theatre, you have discovered a lot about casting that will apply to acting for the camera …that once a company finds an actor who is versatile, well trained, dependable and reliable, they will place that actor in every show they can as often as they can. The reasons are as much for their reliability as for their talent. If you are that actor, you have seen chorus and bit players come and go on a daily basis.

Perhaps you've also noticed that the undisciplined and ill-prepared actors also have the worst attitudes. They are generally late, ill mannered, slovenly, and complain about whatever is most popular to complain about at the time. Conversely, those who are grateful for what they have and speak well of their position and the positions of those around them, are more often than not, given better positions and more opportunities to succeed.

If you are firmly set and prepared with a positive, professional attitude and you have all of your tools current and available, your chances of being asked to sign an agency contract will rise dramatically. Not because they see you as the next Sir Laurence Olivier, but perhaps because there is another local commercial that shoots later this week. Producers are always looking for new faces to fill the background and you may fit that role perfectly.

Keep in mind that the larger the market, the more difficult the signing process becomes, simply because of the increased numbers of actors those agencies are seeing.

"So, if it's so easy to get an agent and the first job, why aren't more doing it?" You ask. Good question. It's not just about the first job…it's about the second job and how you handle each and every job, no matter how large or small. It is this process of *on the job training* that develops or disappoints.

> **Schedule appointments with as many agencies as you are able.**

Before you sign that first contract with that first agent you meet with, commit to interviewing with as many of the agencies in town as is realistically possible.

Put yourself in the mindset that you are shopping. Would you buy the first car you looked at without lifting the hood, taking a test drive or having some warranty to protect you? Why should your career be treated with any less care?

Go to each interview expecting to stay no longer than 15 minutes, even if it took you 2 hours to get there. Take a notebook with you listing these questions:

1. How many actors in my category do you represent?
2. What types of work do they get?

3. On average, how often do they work?

4. Where do you see me fitting in?

5. What are your expectations of me?

6. Where do you see the market as a whole now?

7. Where do you see the market in 5 years?

8. What photographer do you suggest for my next Headshot?

9. What coach or coaches do you recommend I study with?

10. If I follow through on the expectations you've listed for me, what direction or plan do you have in mind for me?

11. Be ready to state your goals and expectations of yourself based on your dream.

Be clear, honest, and professional and thank the agent and the agent's secretary(s) for their time and their interest and mention that you have appointments with (x) number of other agencies and that you intend to fulfill your obligation to meet with them before you make your decision. Gracefully and in a timely manner get out their door and go to the next interview.

> NOTE: Even if you have just interviewed with the last agency on your list, it is important for you to take some time in considering your decision. After all, it is a very important decision. Isn't it?

As soon as you get to your car, immediately write down what you observed. Note how you felt, how you were made to feel and what you learned. First impressions; was the office where you met neat and orderly? How did it feel? How were you treated? Was there eye contact and genuine interest in you? How were your questions treated and answered? Did you respect their time and they yours?

This introductory interview is one where the agent is far busier than you, and they have a million other things on their mind than just you. That is nothing against you; it's just a fact of the business they are in. If they don't get actors roles, they can't pay their bills and will be out of business. So remember to be polite, and most importantly, succinct.

You must be prepared and know that even though this is an extremely important decision for you, to the agent you are one of many.

Later on, as you develop professionally, you will be able to grow your relationship. But for the first interview, just like your most important rule in auditions, ALWAYS leave them wanting more.

Once you have met with all of the agencies on the list, you will have a very good idea as to whom you best connect with. The relationship with an agent is difficult at best!

As you are choosing an agency, remember you must work hard to maintain a positive mutual relationship. Here are some ways to do that:

A mutual trust is essential. If they call you to go to an audition

- be available,
- be prepared,
- always do your best.

You must have a way to show them on a fairly regular basis what you are doing and becoming:

- Always provide your agent with complimentary tickets to shows you are in
- Mail the reviews and promos for everything to your agent's office
- At least twice a year schedule coffee or time to relate to your agent face-to-face what you are doing.

Actors with the Big Fish Talent Agency in Denver are very fortunate to have an agent who provides a bi-monthly opportunity for the actor to show their latest and greatest skills at Sunday afternoon workshop.

Peter DeAnello, Talent Agent for Big Fish Talent Agency, donates his time every other week to come in personally and see each actor who wants to work. (I relieve him every other week not only to allow him personal time, but to give actors a steady and dependable opportunity to get material on its feet and prepare for their work in front of their agent.)

Peter critiques monologues, cold reads and whatever the actors have prepared to work on. I have never known any other agency to ever provide such a diverse opportunity.

NOTE: The Big Fish Talent Agency is currently non-union. Unions are great about protecting their members by not allowing union agencies to have conflicting schools. However, the Sunday night workshops are *drop in* and are free opportunities designed to encourage and stimulate those who attend, to train with professionals and act as a way of learning about and sharing what is going on in the marketplace.

The rented space is paid for when everyone drops a $5.00 donation to share the cost at the door. The workshop space is at the Colorado Film Video Institute where students of the film school can see the actor's work and who then *hire* the actors for their student projects. The benefits are an ever-widening circle of contacts.

Even with that, most actors follow the corporate rule: Twenty percent of the employees do eighty percent of the work. On most Sunday afternoons, the workshop space sees only twenty percent of those who are invited to attend.

The best advice I was ever given by any one in this industry was from Tony Barr, former VP of CBS Dramatic Programming and author of the book entitled *Acting for the Camera*. He said, "Don't ever quit and don't let the bastards wear you down."

The wisdom of his words grows with each encounter and each day that goes by. There have been months when I have made thousands upon thousands of dollars, and months when I wasn't sure if I would ever work again. There were times when casting directors asked for proof of any work; they had no idea who I was. And there were times when everyone I met said, "I saw you in four different commercials back to back last night."

Mike Fenton, co-founder of C.S.A., who at the time I met and worked with him was casting with Jane Feinberg, told stories of how he would have to interview with new directors and convince them he could cast A-list talent. He recounted how the new directors had never heard of him even though he had cast films like *American Graffiti, Young Frankenstein, One Flew Over the Cuckoo's Nest, Raiders of the Lost Ark, E.T.* and more than 200 other such features. That really made an impact. When you think you've done and seen it all, then you probably have, and you should move aside for those still willing to do it.

Okay, so now you are signed with an agent. That agent will have recommended one or several photographers they know who will shoot the look and style that works for the market that agent represents. It's important to select the photographer that is most often recommended by the agents you interviewed with. If every agent mentioned one photographer, you are certain to have found a winner.

Go back now and re-read HEADSHOTS.

Do the same with getting an acting coach. There are as many coaches as there are actors, or so it often seems. For every discipline or focus of the industry, there are coaches who specialize in developing students in those areas of discipline.

There are coaches who specialize in training the student for broadcast commercial work. There are coaches for non-broadcast industrial video and film; coaches for film, for video, and for every discipline the actor will need in order to compete and succeed in the marketplace.

Remember, spend as much time as you can in shopping for the right fit with a coach before you are contracted to stay and pay.

We all tend to do better when we are challenged with new ideas and lessons if we respect the person with whom we are learning.

DOTS SOLUTION:

Did you stay inside the box? Did you take your pencil off the page? If you solved the puzzle correctly, you probably had to try more than once, starting each time by redefining your parameters and then asking yourself how to accomplish the seemingly impossible.

You had to go outside of the box and you had to stay on task and not give up. Likewise, by applying these same virtues to acting, you will accomplish your goals.

Chapter Seventeen

CONCLUSION

I hope that by having read this book, you had some fun and have gained a new perspective of the craft.

As a coach I prefer to think of myself as a slingshot. By using all of my will and my skills when an actor rests her trust and future in my workshops (the sling) it is my goal to propel her far beyond where I am, to the target the actor has set for herself. Reaching the target is the purpose as well as the goal.

What is your target? What is your flight path? It is up to you to make those decisions and then get ready for the ride of your life. You are about to take flight.

Write down your dreams. When you put them on paper, you have taken the first step to realizing their reality.

Write down those things you will need to accomplish your dreams. You have taken one more step closer.

Organize what you wrote into a daily short-term and long-term plan of action. When you assign a date(s) to your plan, you recognize that your dreams are now GOALS.

I encourage you to continue to dream big, smile often and laugh out loud.

You are the creator of your own reality and what you will begin to hear is based on how well you have learned to *LISTEN*.

Your successes will grow in size and frequency as you acknowledge your inner truths which make you *FEEL* more intensely, free and confident.

What you DO each and every day will be more and more important with greater responsibility and reward. That is a great way to live and to *RESPOND*.

GLOSSARY

The language of film and television is like that of any specialized profession. The more terms that you are familiar with the more you will be prepared and relaxed and able to concentrate on things that matter and ignore those that have nothing to do with you.

Since most camera acting workshops are designed to help the actor with how they come across on camera, if a camera is used, it is usually a *video* camera. Film camera language is different from video language. The call sequence is different and after the shot is completed, there are numerous other communications that may sound as though you are suddenly in a foreign land. With this in mind, to better prepare you for your future on camera, I am providing you with a glossary of terms that you will hear or need to know when you arrive on location or on set.

Since most glossaries are pretty stale, I want you to remember that we do this because we love it and usually like to have as much fun as we can, when we can. So to that end, I applaud each of the persons in this great industry who work the long hours for little and often *no pay* to do what they love. Read on.

A

Above the Line Costs Creative and performing personnel. Actors, artists, musicians, writers and associate producers, etc. Also includes offices, studio and rehearsal spaces. Mostly, these costs are on a sliding scale and not always predictable.

A.D. (Assistant Director; Associate Director) A key production assistant who is most often responsible for the timing of the show. The Director assigns their responsibilities and the A.D. is usually the person to whom you will report to when you arrive and will have the most contact with on set. There are often more than one, in which case they are numbered, 1st A.D., 2nd, etc.

A.D.R. (Automated Dialogue Recording) When there is a budget, the dialogue that you worked so hard on to deliver just perfectly on location, will all be re-recorded back at the studio. It can also be referred to as dubbing (at least by us old-timers).

Ad Lib Unrehearsed, spontaneous dialogue and/or action. Often developed through Improvisational training, Ad Lib is very useful in situations that demand that *something extra,* as requested by a director.

Apple box This useful tool is on every set. Much like duct or gaffers tape, it is used for countless reasons. Just as it sounds, it is a wooden box that can be sat upon, used to raise up props, short actors, a camera, or act as a handy dining set at lunchtime. There are also Half and Quarter Apples (This refers to their thickness in comparison to a Full Apple).

Arcing You may be directed to *follow* or to "be aware of the camera that will be arcing around and toward you." This simply means that the camera, which is either mounted on tracks or held by its operator(s), will be moving in a semi-circular motion.

Audio Simply put: Sound. You will often be asked to "settle in, we are going to cut audio." (See "wild sound" and "room tone")

Audit A no-cost or obligation opportunity to sit in on a class or workshop. Usually reserved for new or prospective students.

Audio Booth A room usually not big enough to turn around in, where you will repeat any lines that were not recorded on location due to too much wild sound (A.D.R.), or to record V/O (voice over).

B

Back Light If you were trained in the theatre, you learned early on to *find the light.* Knowing your general light terms is helpful when you are asked to move one way or another toward whatever light the director refers to. The backlight is used to light you from behind to create a better-looking image. (That's always good!)

Below the line costs Technical and production personnel, like camera and audio operators, engineers, as well as production equipment and services and some facilities. Mostly, these costs are fixed rates.

Black In Theatre, it is a black curtain. For camera, the reference is usually, "We will fade to black," or "Fade up from black." In either case, you will be working the scene or the moment, either ad-libbing until you get a cue to start the actual dialogue, or continuing action that is essential to the project until the scene is cut.

Blocking Every piece of equipment, props, set pieces, crew and talent are involved in blocking. Each and every scene is planned out from beginning to end to allow for whatever needs to be seen, as well as things that are to be hidden from the camera, as the scene is played out.

Boom A long armed device that suspends a microphone held just out of frame to capture your dialogue. Often held by a well-toned professional (the more lines you have the more toned the professional).

Bounce Card Usually a white or silver piece of cloth or foam core used to bounce light onto the subject being photographed. (It is reassuring to know this the first time you hear they are going to have to use a bounce card. It does not mean you will be given your walking papers.)

C

C.G. (Character Generator) Generally, when you are hired to work commercials or industrials, the director will ask you to look at specific points where they will "C.G." phone numbers, etc. At the time of production you may be looking at a dot stuck on a wall or on a C-Stand, but in post, the editor will electronically insert images that make it appear as though you can see the numbers or objects that you were seeing as a dot in production.

C-Stand This universal tool is used to hold lights, clothing, or to prop up an exhausted technician. Specifically it is a silver metal stand with telescoping height, an arm that swings to any position and stabilizing legs that fold flat when not in use.

Call This word deserves two definitions. The first would be your **call time**. Generally you would arrive 10 minutes before your call time but never earlier than that and certainly never after that. The second definition would be when the series of calls are made to start the filming of a scene. "**Call it**" followed by "Roll Sound, …Roll Camera, …Mark it," …then, "Action." An actor needs to be aware, and in concentrated preparation for when *Action* is called to then deliver accordingly.

Catwalk Unless you are playing a villain in a superhero picture, the catwalk is a series of walkways and pipes where equipment and lighting is suspended, near the ceiling of the studio.

Cheat Just as when you cheated on a test, the object was not to get caught. When you cheat for the camera the same rule applies. You can cheat (move) a prop, set piece or a performer to make the shot look better or to emphasize a particular element in the scene as long as the eye or the camera believes it. For actors, at auditions, you should always cheat to the camera.

Chroma key More often referred to as "Green Screen." This technical aid is used regularly by meteorologists showing changing weather patterns on the daily news programs. Working in front of a green (or sometimes blue) wall, it can appear that you are anywhere but in the studio. You may have seen it used on *Whose Line Is It Anyway*, with Drew Carey.

Clapper No, this is not the device you bought to turn your lights on and off. It is used to sync sound on a take by clapping two sticks together. See: Slate or Clapboard.

Clap board See: Slate. *(Just like your yellow pages, isn't it?)*

Close-Up As in, "I am ready for my Close-up, Mr. DeMille." This is a shot that features mainly the face, when dealing with a person.

Collective Shot Also referred to as an Establishing Shot, in which the relationship of character to setting and/or time or other elements are shown in the frame.

Continuity A critical part of any picture. Whether it is seen or heard, whenever the camera changes angles or locations, whatever was seen or heard must match with what was seen or heard in the previous shot. i.e. the water level in the glass, the cigarette, the angle of the light shining in the window, the level of light, sound and anything else you see and hear.

Control Room In a studio, this room is where the video signals are controlled, and often where the director or technical director controls all of the elements of the shoot.

Cookie Don't call your attorney. The Gaffer who is asking for a cookie is neither asking for you, nor is he hungry. A cookie is either metal or wood (or some other material) that is put in front of a lighting instrument that filters the light to appear as though the light is shining through leaves, trees, window frames or some pattern of light and shadow (The full name for a cookie is Cucalorous, but is also nicknamed Kook).

Cover Shot See: Establishing Shot.

Coverage Just when you think the director missed the part of your scene they think they should have gotten now, he will tell you that they will pick it up in coverage. Scripts are broken down into shots and how those shots will be edited together is described as coverage. (Time, budget and lighting and location have a lot to do with how the shots are established and shot.)

Cross-Fade A technically controlled effect used to fade out picture and/or sound while simultaneously fading in new picture and/or sound. This is where it is important that you hold your emotion or, if directed, continue your action or dialogue until you are clear of the effect.

Cue To give a signal to the actor or technician to start (and/or end) the performance, action or effect.

Cue-to-Cue Rehearsal Omitting most lines and a lot of blocking, this rehearsal will familiarize cast and crew with the overall run of the show.

Cut This universal word is used in all 3 phases of production. In Pre-Production, Cut refers to the plan of where and when shots will be ended. In Production it can mean CUT! (Please, stop everything! This actor can't put two words together!) Or Cut! (This actor is AWESOME! A one-take wonder!) Finally, in Post Production, the editor is asked to cut the scene at certain points.

Cutaway This term applies to a shot that visually emphasizes the subject matter in a new shot that will be added in post. It is usually a close-up or a descriptive landscape inserted to help move the storyline.

Cyc Pronounced like *psych*. Iinterestingly enough, cyc is a set dressing designed to *psych* you into believing you are seeing something other than just a cloth drape. Often, it is a huge piece of painted or colored draping that is lit and made to look like sky and or landscape or any number of things. The largest or longest, continuous cyc used in film history was in Rick Ramage's 2004 film, *Ichabod*! It was 504 feet in length, constructed of six panels 84 feet wide and 23 feet long. By the way, Cyc is short for Cyclorama and psych is short for psychology. Whoopdedoo.

D

Director This person is the one you want to befriend, get to know, send chocolates to and so forth. The director has the overall vision and responsibility for the picture and sound throughout the production and postproduction.

Dissolve Here is another technically produced transition (done in post) where the actor is often directed to either continue his action or "hold" while the picture and sound "dissolve."

Dolly A dolly move is nowhere as cute as it sounds (unless you think the camera operator is a "doll"). It is simply the movement of the camera (and whatever it is mounted on) closer to, or further away from its subject. A "dolly shot" can also be referred to as a "tracking shot" although somewhat incorrectly, as a tracking shot may also include side-to-side movement (For definition of side to side movement, see "Trucking").

Dress Rehearsal If you are so fortunate as to have a dress rehearsal, it is the time for both cast and crew to have a run-through of the scene or scenes with all sets, props and etc., preferably without stopping to get a feel for how it looks, sounds and feels, overall.

Dry Run One hot, summer day, I strapped on my running shoes…never mind. A dry run is another type of rehearsal, usually without camera or other technical additives.

Dutch Tilt This is not an offering for a cold, adult beverage. It is the way a camera operator will adjust the camera to angle left or right of center to give a unique and somewhat uncomfortable look to the frame.

E

Edit Editing is the act of putting the film or video together from its many parts and pieces into one continuous and effective storyline. (Post-Production)

Effects You may see this on a script as "FX" or "SFX" which stands for "Special Effects." See: Special Effects. (Because it's just too much work to type the definition twice!)

Ellipsoidal Spotlight Don't you just love the way that phrase rolls off your tongue? Well, so do gaffers, so they call it a Leko *(lee-ko)*. This lighting instrument is used a lot to define special lighting with metal shutters that open or close, allowing more or less light, and often with a cookie.

Establishing Shot Just like the name implies, this shot establishes setting, relationships, etc. It is usually wide and takes in the whole of the location in which the scene will take place.

Extemporaneous For those of you who had this speaking class in your formal education, you already know. For the rest of you, it can be shortened to simply "B.S." See: Improvisation.

Eye Line Wrong-o, this is not a Maybelline moment. Your eye line is the direction in which you are told to look off-camera so that as the camera angle is changed, your look remains consistent (Also see: Continuity). Your eye line can be set with a piece of gaff tape on a C-stand or your off-camera scene partner.

F

Fade Something we all do after a very long and arduous day of shooting. However in film language, it is another example of a scene transition created by the editor in post. A *fade in* means the picture comes up and in from black; a *fade out* means the picture goes down and out to black.

Feed Besides the obvious comestibles, a feed is the program signal (picture/video and sound/audio) that is brought in, from an outside source, to the studio.

Feedback We have all heard the feedback from an audio source, creating that high-pitched squeal that even your baby sister can't compete with. Generally, from a microphone that is live receiving a monitor signal at the same time. Video feedback is created when the same video signal is re introduced into the same switcher.

Flex-Fill These things are great. Used just like a bounce card, they are round pieces of white or silver cloth on a heavy wire frame that folds up into a small, tight little package when not in use. You may have seen a similar item used to pop-up and put in your dash/windshield to protect your car's interior from the hot sun.

Flag No need to place your hand over your heart. These are thick, heavy black pieces of cloth stretched over a hard frame and are used to block light from being in the shot, or from creating a flare in the camera lens. In a pinch anything that blocks light can be used as a flag. There is another definition that describes what film editors use when they want to easily locate a place on the film reel. As a reel of film is being wound onto its spool, the technician will place a piece of tape or paper (also called a flag) on the film roll.

Flare Although you see these warning devices used along roadside accidents, the term flare in film and video work refers to the foggy or streaking look you see when light shines directly into the camera lens.

Foley Not only is this the name for sound effects added to film and video soundtracks, but it is more importantly the recognition of the man who created the art; Jack Foley. Foley effects are produced by a Foley artist who watches the picture and matches the action, adding appropriate sound, like footsteps, doors opening and closing, etc.

Frame It's true, actors enjoy being framed. A frame is one image (among many in a long piece of film) that creates motion. There are 24 frames that are exposed every second in film and 31 per second in video.

French Flag Once again, no need to salute. This tidy little unit is a small, square or rectangular piece of flat, black metal that is mounted on a flex arm and then onto a camera to block light or stop flares in the lens.

F-stop When you get a technician placing a light meter in your face looking at its readings, they are going to set the F-stop based on what they learn from the light meter. See: Light Meter. The F-stop is the measurement used to decide what the opening of the iris should be, which decides how much light is allowed to expose the film

Gaffer Brits refer to old people as gaffers; however, in the motion picture industry, we know them as the head of the lighting department.

Gaffers' Tape (Gaffe Tape) Man, you thought duct tape was expensive! Similar in size to duct tape, gaffe tape is usually black but comes in silver too. The best part is, it doesn't leave that (nasty) sticky stuff when you pull it off. Everyone should have a roll.

Gel You already have enough gel in your hair. This gel refers to a large, colored, plastic sheet that is placed in front of lighting instruments or to filter light from windows. A blue gel is often used for moonlight, orange, for evening light, etc.

Gobo If you know what a cookie is, you know what this is. (Where DO they come up with this stuff?)

Graphics Unless you are given artwork to show on camera (that can also be referred to as graphics) most graphics are created in post. See: "C.G." Graphics are charts, photos, maps, etc.

Grip These people are rarely seen sitting still. A grip is assigned mostly to move scenery and set dressings like furniture, plants, etc. but they are usually doing many other tasks as well.

H

Handheld You might be on a moonlit romantic stroll, but the camera is not on a tripod or mount, it is being handheld by its operator.

Hanging Mike Just because you don't like him…Okay, it's a microphone that is hanging from somewhere out of camera range.

Head You have one; the camera attaches to one on a tripod, and the beginning of a scene or shot is called one as well.

Headroom M-M-M-Max, Headroom. (If you are too young, you may not get that one.) Anyhow, headroom is the space between the top of your head and the top of the frame. As with most things, too much or too little is not good.

Headset Most of us have these on our phones now, but technicians use them to speak to and hear each other during production.

Hi Hat This definition begs an apology. The device called a *hi hat* is a square board with a tripod head bolted to it, allowing the operator to mount the camera very low to the ground. The name *hi hat* stuck from the time it was first designed for use on *high* mountings.

HMI (Halogen Metal Incandescence) These babies are BRIGHT. They are also heavy and expensive. These rather large lights require a ballast to operate, which makes them even heavier. The payoff is they make great light.

High Key Lighting Like you were outside! It is a bright overall lighting from above and the background has as much light on it. Often this kind of lighting is used when you are doing chroma-key work.

Hot Set When you see this sign on the door or entrance to a studio or location, it marks a set where everything on it must be left exactly where it is. The cast and crew are on break and will be returning to shoot more on the same set.

I

Incandescent Light Just like the 60-watt bulb you replaced last week, these lights operate when the metal filament is heated to glowing.

Indies Though they may not have the last name, "Jones", they all hope to make the next big blockbuster. They are the Independent filmmakers.

Insert edit That's right, just like it sounds. An insert is where a new piece of film or video is electronically added to an existing piece.

Insert Shot You got it. An insert is usually a close-up added to create emphasis. (Much like a cutaway.)

Iris A beautiful flower, but the iris to which we are referring allows just the right amount of light into the camera. When you are a spokesperson talking right into the lens, you will see the iris open and close. (You'll get used to it.)

J

Jack This is a receptacle or socket that an audio connector is plugged into. (Female). It is also a hinged brace on the backside of a stage flat.

Jump Cut Usually not a good idea. When the same subject is photographed from two different angles and then edited together. When the edit rolls, the subject appears to *jump*.

K

K You shouldn't have any trouble spelling this word! This letter is used quite often by gaffers and lighting techs. Like, "Get me that 12k HMI." That's when you ask if you can go put on more deodorant. It's gonna' get HOT! One k is 1,000 watts but it takes just over 5,000k to measure sunlight.

Key Picture in a picture that is added and removed electronically.

Key Light This is the one that can blind you. It is the primary source of light that shines right at you and in order to deal with shadows they have to use other lights or distance you from anything your shadow will fall on. (Unless they need to see your shadow!)

Kicker Usually added to balance out the key light, the kicker is an additional light to the rear and side of the subject being photographed.

Kill In addition to the command you give to your pit bull, this word is used to turn off equipment.

Kook See Cookie. Or anyone you choose to so label.

L

Land A lot of actors are also real estate agents and they usually buy and sell land. However, to *land* is to *end up* or to *stop* on a predetermined spot or mark.

Lavaliere A small microphone that can be easily hidden under your lapel.

Lead Room Nope, this is not where the stars hang out. It is the amount of room you have between you and the edge of frame as you move about. It is also referred to as *nose room*.

Leko See: Ellipsoidal Spotlight.

Lens What needs to be defined here? It is what you look into or you avoid looking into depending on what you are doing and how you are directed.

Level When you are asked to give a level, you won't have to reach into your pockets; you should deliver your lines just as you will when you are at performance level. The sound engineer is then able to set the recording level of your voice.

Lighting Grid Look up. Those rows and rows of pipes are what lights are hung on.

Light Meter This is a handheld device that gets put next to your face to measure the light that reflects off of it. Now they can set the iris on the camera.

Limbo If you ever feel like you are in limbo, you may well be! Limbo is a set with little, if anything, on it.

Line Supervisor Your best friend or enemy, depending on how prepared you are. See: Continuity. This person corrects any lines or words you may have missed in your delivery.

Lock Down Shot The camera is locked down where it will not move. Great stuff for making it appear someone can disappear!

Lock it down. This command is given before shooting to secure all noise or distraction from becoming a part of the shot. So settle!

Long Shot (LS) When you are a great distance from the camera, they are using a long lens and you can still be heard as though they are right next to you. (So watch what you say. As always.)

Looping See A.D.R.; it is similar, but the difference is the film that you are adding your voice to is on a loop, so you have numerous opportunities to get it right.

M

Mark When you are asked to "hit your Mark," it is not an invitation to start a fight. A mark can be a piece of tape placed on the floor showing where the actor should stand or land.

"Mark it" Once everyone is set for the shot, this command is given to whomever is running marker or sticks to have them place the clapboard in front of the camera lens to mark the scene and the audio by clapping the sticks together. (**Note:** Many clapboards are now digital and mark the scene electronically.)

Master Shot Typically, the master shot is wide and is shot first, to establish setting, characters, etc. Pick up shots are then edited to match with the master shot.

Matte This shot is sort of like Chroma-Key, only you don't need a green or blue background. The cameras are set up so that one is foreground and the other background.

Medium Shot (MS) When you see this abbreviation on your script, now you will know it's generally between a close-up and a long shot.

Moiré Effect You know that striped pattern shirt or tight checked jacket you love so much? Forget wearing them on camera if you are to appear on TV. They will look like they are alive. The pattern will interact with the electronic scan lines and go whacko!

Monitor Either a speaker and/or video screen that will give you an idea of what is going to be seen, heard or broadcast. It is a huge help when your show is live.

M.O.S. You will see this quite often on your script, and hear it through direction to cast and crew. Legend has it that it was started when a German director called the shot "without sound" but of course, sounded like "Mit Out Sound."

N

Nose Room See Lead room. More specifically though, this refers to the on-camera talent's profile and the distance to the edge of frame.

O

Objective Perspective Use of the camera as the observer or eavesdropper, where no one addresses the camera.

Off Camera Often, the performer is asked to start his lines or action off camera. (Easy, huh.) You may see it on your script marked as OS. Meaning: Off Screen.

Omni directional (Non directional) This microphone picks up sound from all directions. As opposed to a unidirectional mic.

Outtakes Footage that is not used in the final project. Footage only editors, directors and select talent and crew were once able to see; now anyone who selects the DVD Special Features can judge for themselves whether the footage was worthy or not.

Over crank This produces a faster—than-normal speed of film through the camera, thus rendering a slower-than-normal movement on screen. To photograph a speeding bullet, you either need Superman with a steadicam or over crank.

Over the Shoulder Shot (O/S) The camera is using one actor's head and shoulder to frame the other facing them.

P

Pad Extra video and or audio that are used to *fill* or extend the program.

Pan The movement of the camera on its mount from left to right, or right to left.

Pigeon A hi hat for lights. I once overheard a direction "Get me a pigeon from the cage." I was much relieved to find they wanted to mount a light lower than any light stand would go.

Pix Abbreviation for Picture(s). The use of the word always reminds me of the scene in Yankee Doodle Dandy where Cagney explains the Variety headline. (Find it in chapter 33 of the DVD.)

Playback Watch the monitor after having completed a shot. The V.T.R. operator will rewind the scene as it was recorded and provide *playback* showing what was recorded on film or video.

Pop Filter This device looks like a screen or stretched woven fiber that keeps hard consonants from *popping* on the recording. It softens p's and t's.

Post Production Once the filming is completed, the film or video and audio segments are sent to be edited into the final feature.

Potentiometer (pot) A knob or slider that controls volume. Now when you hear one tech tell another "pot up" you won't be thinking the wrong thing.

P.O.V. (Point Of View) Shot Used to show the viewer what the character sees. Usually followed by a reaction shot that expresses the feeling intended.

Practical This is not a judgment on anyone. It is a light that is used in the picture. Example: A table lamp or whatever lights you, as the character, may be using in the scene. You may be asked to turn on or off the practical.

Preproduction This period of time is when all of the planning that can be done before filming is done. It is a well known fact that the more time that is spent in preproduction, the less time will be needed in production, with far better results.

Preroll Extra time on camera when film is being exposed before the actual start of the scene. You should be in character and ready for whatever direction is given.

Presence When you are given or asked to give more presence, there is a need to have more of your voice. Usually an intimate, deeper or even breathier sound.

Producer The creator as well as originator of most TV programs and motion pictures. The producer is usually in charge of all the above-the-line elements. (See Above-the-line costs)

Properties (Props) Items that are moved used and handled easily.

Proscenium (Proscenium Arch) This is the furthest downstage section that separates the auditorium from the stage. Don't fall off!

Pull Focus (Rack Focus) If there are two subjects in frame, one closer than the other, this technique is employed by the focus puller and camera operator to change the focus from the near subject to the far and vice versa.

Q

Quartz Light These babies will blind you! The filament is made of tungsten-halogen and is in a quartz or silica housing. They are used a lot for their efficiency. I guess you may not care, but it was the only Q definition I could think of.

R

Rack Focus See "Pull Focus."

Reaction Shot A performer's (literal) reaction. A reaction shot usually precedes or immediately follows a P.O.V. shot. It may be shot M.O.S.

Ready This word at least used to be the standard command used just prior to calling "Action" or just prior to "cut." I suppose it still is when shots are being called from control, but now it seems I hear … "And" more often in place of "ready."

Reverse Shot After establishing, a reverse shows the other side. This generally means moving the camera and relighting; however, if the scene is set in limbo, it may be the actors who reverse, saving lots of time.

Room Tone Recording the sound of the space without any extraneous noise or dialogue. (Bite your tongue for 30 seconds!)

Rough Cut Just like it sounds, it is *rough*. This is the first completed edit. There are no fancy transitions, either with picture or sound.

Rushes Also known as "dailies," it is the work print that has been returned from the lab, unedited and meant only to prove that everything came out okay. (Or not).

S

Safety You may hear, "One more for safety." Unless someone on crew is named Safety, you are going to give one more just to be sure. (Note "One" is rarely just one.)

Scanning The electron beams in both the video camera and the video monitor have a pattern that are horizontal and run from top to bottom. (See Moiré for more information why knowing this is fun.)

Scene (One of the most abused words in the industry.) A scene as defined by the theatre would require more than one setup or one shot for camera. That is why a *sequence* of shots is what is defined as a scene for camera.

Segue *Seg-way* Originally intended only as a reference of one portion of audio fading out as the next is faded in, it now is used as another word for an opening transition between one thought and the next, either visually or verbally.

Sharpie Like gaffe tape, no production is complete without these beauties. A permanent ink pen made by the Sanford Company that is used to mark film canisters, the film itself and that hot P.A.'s number on your forearm.

Shot Unless you are a postal NRA member, it refers to exposed film or recorded information from "Action" to "Cut."

Slate 1. Your introduction on camera when you audition. It includes your name, agency affiliation and union affiliation, although union affiliation is not always required or asked for. Also, if you are a child, it may include your age. 2. The board, which marks information for the editor about the shot. It often includes the clapper with which to mark the shot.

S.M.P.T.E. Society of Motion Picture and Television Engineers. *(Often referred to as "Sim-Tees")* These folks got together and decided they needed one, universal code that would be understood without a rocket science degree, by all technicians in the film and video arts. By using the SMPTE time code, you can locate any frame or any section of video by hour, minute, second or frame! (Now if we could just get them to work on computer compatibility, or wire connectors or ...)

SOF Sound On Film. Next time you see that on your script, you'll know what it means. It refers to the film sound track.

Speed Used to acknowledge that sound and camera are rolling and recording as they should; the Director is assured it is safe to call "Action."

Spike Many of these are used to hold the rails to the ties. Wait a minute. This is not about railroads ...though in the theatre, spikes are used to mark where furniture and props are to be located on a set, so they can be replaced precisely where they were first established.

Sticks If the person asking for sticks is holding a camera, they mean a tripod. If they are standing behind the camera and "roll camera" or "roll tape" has been called, they are asking for a clapboard marker to be sounded. If they are sitting at a drum set ...never mind, that's another book too.

Stinger I have no idea how an "extension cord" became a "stinger," but will somebody PLEASE unplug this thing? It's killing me!

Steadicam This device allows a camera operator to hold and carry the camera steady, as they follow whatever action they are shooting.

Super 16 Lots of Indies are using this type of film because it is less expensive than the larger format, 35mm film and can be blown up to a 35mm print if necessary. It has the sprocket holes on only one side of the film, giving it more room for image where the soundtrack would ordinarily be.

Superimposition *(Super, as an abbreviation)* When titles are put in the frame or other graphics.

Sync *(abbreviation for Synchronize)* Picture and sound must be in sync. But that does not mean you need a popular recording group to do it.

T

Tail Slate 1. You will repeat your audition slate when you complete your on-camera read. 2. After shooting a setup, the clapper is turned upside down and placed on camera and marked to clarify shot end.

Take 1. When there is a multi-camera set up, the director will call which camera is live with "take." It is an instant change from one camera to the other, and so on. 2. Numerous shots of the same scene or setup; each is considered a "take." Take it away!

Talent Any person who appears in front of the camera. Don't get cocky, though. The people behind the camera have a lot of talent too!

Tilt If you tilt, it is probably to one side or the other; however if it is a camera that is tilting, it is either an up or down direction on its axis (or head).

Time Lapse Have you ever seen a flower sprout, bloom, shrivel and die all in less than 10 seconds? (Probably) But someone had to lockdown their camera and the planter for the flower, regulate the lighting and take a very large number of short takes over a long period of time to make that happen. Time sure can fly. (At least for the viewer.)

Tracking Shot Also See "Dolly" and "Trucking." The camera and its mount are on tracks and are able to follow (moving with) the movement of the talent as the segment is shot.

Transmitter When you are wired with a lavaliere, the transmitter is that black box with a little wire (antenna) on it (or in it) at the other end of the wire from the little microphone. Be sure to turn it off or ask to have it turned off before leaving set for any reason. There are plenty of stories about those who haven't.

Trucking As we used to say in the 70's, "Keep on trucking." Trucking is simply the movement of the entire camera mount laterally to the left or right.

U

Under crank Things just moving too slow for ya? Remedy: Under crank. That is, to slow the camera speed down so that when the film or video is played back, it appears to move faster. **Note:** Early films were shot at 18 fps (frames per second) and many projectionists over cranked the projectors and viewers got used to it. Now we almost expect to see *oldies* running a bit too fast and jerky.

Unidirectional (Cardiod) This microphone picks up sound from only one direction (as opposed to the omni directional mic.). It just so happens that the direction is actually a heart shape, therefore it's called "cardiod."

V

Vault Box It holds the film, so keep them safe and secure!

Video What you *see* (or the visual portion) of a Television program.

VTR Video Tape Recorder. The video assist on a film shoot allows for instant playback; however the digital revolution may soon replace VTRs with tapeless recorders.

W

Walk-Through Rehearsal These rehearsals are great to get familiar with the overall run of a show without having to run all of the lines and/or technical moves. More detailed than just a cue-to-cue.

Wild Sound Sound information gathered (or recorded) by the sound engineer without the camera rolling. (Also see "Room Tone")

Wipe Yeah, sort of like that. A transition of one image to the next with a horizontal, vertical or diagonal movement.

Wrap Both the best and worst word to hear. After a long, difficult and exhausting day, it is good to hear, "Let's wrap for the day." When that same shoot is finished and you hear, "That's a wrap," you are out of another job and you will wonder what to do with yourself tomorrow when you wake up at 3 a.m. with no call time. (Get over it and use the time to prepare for your next audition!)

X

Xenon Warrior Princess (not really, just kidding) These types of lamps require specific equipment housings and different lab processing when shooting color film, all because they are considered for daylight temperature.

Y

Y not? I can't think of a thing that starts with Y that you would need or want to know. But I just hated not to at least honor the letter.

Z

Zoom In To change a zoom lens to a narrow angle from wide to better emphasize the subject being photographed.

Zoom Lens This lens will allow for a smooth change of focus as it is moved from distant to close subjects and vice versa.

Zoom Out (or Back) To go from a long focal length (narrow angle) to a wide angle (short focal length).

*   *   *

You are welcome to visit me at www.rohreringsuccess.com. I look forward to hearing from you.

Paul Neal Rohrer

978-0-595-35170-1
0-595-35170-0

Made in the USA
Columbia, SC
15 November 2021

49019086R00093